Central and Eastern European Development Studies

Markus Leibenath · Ewa Korcelli-Olejniczak ·
Robert Knippschild

Cross-border Governance and Sustainable Spatial Development

Mind the Gaps!

With 12 Figures and 5 Tables

Springer

Dr. Markus Leibenath
Leibniz Institute of Ecological
and Regional Development
Weberplatz 1
01217 Dresden
Germany
M.Leibenath@ioer.de

Dr. Ewa Korcelli-Olejniczak
PAN Warsaw
Institute of Geography and
Spatial Organization
ul. Twarda 51/55
00-818 Warsaw
Poland
eko@twarda.pan

Dr. Robert Knippschild
Leibniz Institute of Ecological
and Regional Development
Weberplatz 1
01217 Dresden
Germany
R.Knippschild@ioer.de

ISBN: 978-3-540-79243-7

e-ISBN: 978-3-540-79244-4

Library of Congress Control Number: 2008926103

Cover design: deblik, Berlin

Printed on acid-free paper

9 8 7 6 5 4 3 2 1

springer.com

Preface

The relevance of borders is particularly high in Central Europe because hardly any other part of the world features a comparable density of sovereign states. While the number of states is continuously growing since the political watershed of 1990, a far-reaching process of integration and Europeanization is taking place – epitomized by successive rounds of enlarging the European Union. Parallel to these phenomena of bordering and rebordering, of separation and of integration, border regions undergo tremendous changes. The book explores the consequences of these processes for cross-border governance and spatial planning in Central Europe.

The contributions are based on presentations given at an international workshop which was organized in Warsaw in the frame of the German-Polish Year 2006 in Poland and in cooperation with spa-ce.net, the Network of Spatial Research and Planning Institutes in Central and Eastern Europe. The editors wish to thank the Institute of Geography and Spatial Organization of the Polish Academy of Sciences, Warsaw, and the Leibniz Institute of Ecological and Regional Development, Dresden, for the supportive environment and the spirit of cooperation which made this event possible in the first place. The editors also thank the German Federal Ministry for Education and Science who co-financed the workshop.

The editors are sincerely grateful to the series editors Bernhard Müller and Wilfried Erbguth for their support, to Rhodes Barrett for eliminating all sorts of linguistic errors from the manuscript and finally to Margitta Wahl for transferring the manuscript into a printable format.

Dresden and Warsaw, March 2008

Markus Leibenath, Ewa Korcelli-Olejniczak and Robert Knippschild

Contents

Exploring the gaps: Sustainability as a challenge for cross-border governance in Central Europe
Markus Leibenath 1

I External influences and framework conditions

Implications of spatial development policies at European and national levels for border regions: The case of Germany
Manfred Miosga 15

Implementation of the EU Community Initiative INTERREG III A at the Polish-German border: An attempt at evaluation
Stanisław Ciok and Andrzej Raczyk 33

II Cross-border governance at regional level

Cross-border co-operation in the Rhine-Scheldt Delta: The long road of institution building
Jochem de Vries 51

Social capital and other main influences on governance processes in cross-border micro-regions: The case of the Austrian-German Euregio 'Via Salina'
Sonja Deppisch 67

III Cross-border co-operation between cities and metropolitan regions

Cross-border cooperation challenges: Positioning the Vienna-Bratislava region
Matej Jaššo 87

Inter-urban cooperation in the German-Polish-Czech triangle
Robert Knippschild 101

Functional complementarity as basis for inter-metropolitan collaboration and networking: A case study on cultural activities in Berlin and Warsaw
Ewa Korcelli-Olejniczak 117

IV Sectoral perspectives on border regions

Transborder transport: The case of Poland's present and future Schengen area boundaries
Tomasz Komornicki 133

Sustainable tourism development in cross-border biosphere reserves of Central and Eastern Europe
Birgit Nolte 147

Environmental dimension of transboundary spatial development – driving forces in environmental regionalism: A case study on the Polish-German borderland
Marek Degórski 161

The role of special economic zones in the socio-economic development of Poland's border regions: The case of the Kostrzyn-Słubice Special Economic Zone
Michał Dolata 175

V Conclusions

Bridging the gaps? – Cross-border governance between top-down policies and local needs and limitations
Markus Leibenath, Ewa Korcelli-Olejniczak and Robert Knippschild 187

Contributing authors

Ciok, Stanisław, Prof. Dr.
Department of Spatial Planning, Institute for Geography and Regional Development
University of Wrocław
pl. Uniwersytecki 1, 50-137 Wrocław, Poland
ciok@geogr.uni.wroc.pl

De Vries, Jochem, Dr.
Faculty of Social and Behavioural Sciences, University of Amsterdam
Nieuwe Prinsengracht 130, 1018 VZ Amsterdam, The Netherlands
jochemdevries@xs4all.nl

Degórski, Marek, Prof. Dr.
Institute of Geography and Spatial Organisation, Polish Academy of Sciences
Twarda 51/55, 00-818 Warsaw, Poland
m.degor@twarda.pan.pl

Deppisch, Sonja, Dr.
Martin-Luther-Platz 11a, D-01099 Dresden, Germany
s_deppisch@yahoo.de

Dolata, Michał, Dr.
Institute of Socio-Economic Geography and Spatial Management, University of Poznań
Ul. Dzięgielowa 27, 61-680 Poznań, Poland
dolata@amu.edu.pl

Jaššo, Matej, Dr.
Institute of Spatial Plannign and Urban Design, Faculty of Architecture
Slovak University of Technology
Nam. Slobody 19, 81245 Bratislava, Slovakia
jasso@fa.stuba.sk

Knippschild, Robert, Dr.
Leibniz-Institute for Ecological and Regional Development
Weberplatz 1, 01217 Dresden, Germany
R.Knippschild@ioer.de

Komornicki, Tomasz, Dr.
Institute of Geography and Spatial Organisation, Polish Academy of Sciences
Twarda 51/55, 00-818 Warsaw, Poland
t.komorn@twarda.pan.pl

Korcelli-Olejniczak, Ewa, Dr.
Institute of Geography and Spatial Organisation, Polish Academy of Sciences
Twarda 51/55, 00-818 Warsaw, Poland
eko@twarda.pan.pl

Leibenath, Markus, Dr.
Leibniz-Institute for Ecological and Regional Development
Weberplatz 1, 01217 Dresden, Germany
M.Leibenath@ioer.de

Miosga, Manfred, Dr.
Identität & Image Coaching AG
Argelsrieder Feld 1b, 82234 Weßling, Germany
Manfred.Miosga@t-online.de

Nolte, Birgit, Dr.
Institute for Geography, University of Greifswald
Makarenkostraße 22, 17487 Greifswald, Germany
bnolte@uni-greifswald.de

Raczyk, Andrzej, Dr.
Department of Spatial Planning, Institute for Geography and Regional Development
University of Wrocław
pl. Uniwersytecki 1, 50-137 Wrocław, Poland
andrzej.raczyk@geogr.uni.wroc.pl

Exploring the gaps

Sustainability as a challenge for cross-border governance in Central Europe

Markus Leibenath

Leibniz Institute of Ecological and Regional Development, Dresden

1 Mind the gaps! – By the way, which gaps?

Research on border regions and cross-border cooperation is essentially concerned with gaps: how gaps emerge and vanish, what effects they have, and how people deal with them.

When looking at national borders in Central Europe, various kinds of gaps can be identified. There are still significant economic disparities between countries, between East and West, and between metropolitan and peripheral regions. The diversity of cultures and institutions that becomes particularly evident at borders can be regarded either as another case of gaps or as one of the major assets of the European continent. There are also cleavages between the perspectives of actors from different policy sectors and different levels of policy-making. For instance, an official from the European Commission's Directorate-General for Energy and Transport views borders differently than an activist from a local environmental NGO.

Furthermore, there are gaps between rhetoric and reality, e.g., when it comes to issues such as sustainability or the integration of the European continent. For instance, the German government traditionally describes itself as the vanguard of integration, but has negotiated transition agreements that restrict the access of Polish and Czech workers to the German labour market for up to 12 years. Or there is much talk about the need to cooperate across borders and harmonize spatial plans, but the conditions on the ground are often sobering. Many more gaps could be described, e.g.

between past, present and future – keeping in mind the dynamic developments that have taken place in Central Europe since political regime change in 1989/1990.

The focus of this book is on cross-border governance and sustainable spatial development in Central Europe. The intention is to explore the gaps between different border regions and approaches to cross-border governance in Central Europe, as well as between different disciplinary perspectives on borders. The aim is to shed light on some current research on border regions and cross-border cooperation and eventually to identify knowledge gaps and needs for further research.

The volume is based on presentations given at the international workshop "Towards Sustainable Border Regions. Analyses, Strategies and Approaches for Transboundary Spatial Development". This event was organized jointly by the Institute of Geography and Spatial Organisation of the Polish Academy of Sciences and the Leibniz Institute of Ecological and Regional Development in the frame of the German-Polish year in Poland. The participants were mostly young researchers, many of whom were affiliated with the Network of Spatial Research and Planning Institutes in Central and Eastern Europe (spa-ce.net).

Although a certain bias towards Poland and Germany cannot be denied, the geographic scope of the book is principally open. It includes case studies from borders between countries such as Austria, Belgium, the Czech Republic, Hungary, the Netherlands, and Slovakia.

A brief introduction to the issues of borders and sustainability is followed by an outline of the structure of the book.

2 New borders in a new Europe

Since the end of the Cold War, the number of sovereign states and hence the length of borders has increased significantly in Europe. Considering only Central and Eastern European countries that have acceded to the European Union in 2004, 6 of the 10 new Member States did not exist 20 years ago: Estonia, Latvia, Lithuania, the Czech Republic, Slovakia, and Slovenia.

The recent EU enlargement has increased the length of internal land borders by 174 per cent while the EU external border has increased by only 23 per cent and the population by 20 per cent. Today more than half EU's internal land borders – roughly 16,500 kilometres – are to be found in the new Member States. If one defines border regions as NUTS-3-territories adjacent to a national border, then 66 per cent of the area of the new Member Sates can be regarded as border region containing 57 per cent of the population in comparison to 21 and 15 per cent respectively in the EU as a whole (Schindegger et al. 2005: 5-8).

These figures make clear that border regions are an important spatial category in Europe. But what is the character of borders as such? What does the term border actually mean? And what forces influence the nature of European borders at the beginning of the 21st century? – It is obvious that the enlargement of the EU, but also the entire process of Europeanization, which concerns all Member States, is fundamentally changing the function and the effects of borders. At the new external borders, the Schengen regime with its strict border controls has to be implemented. By contrast, the new internal borders are becoming less of an obstacle to the flows of people, services, goods, and investment. But Europeanization means more than implementing these famous four freedoms. It is also about the evolution and adoption of the *acquis communautaire*, including various sectoral policies with cross-border effects, e.g., transport or environment, and about access to EU funding schemes for border regions. These policies affect the borders of all Member States.

Other major factors that influence the character of European borders are the overarching and often subtle processes of rescaling and re-territorializing. Rescaling economic activities refers to the phenomenon of globalization. Re-territorializing means the shift of powers away from the level of national governments to sub-national units (regionalization), but also to supranational organisations (Perkman & Sum 2002: 11). The emerging new forms of multi-level governance include a broad range of non-governmental actors like private companies and NGOs.

What does this imply for border regions and for the character of European borders? – At least four trajectories of change can be identified:

- First, EU enlargement leads to higher permeability of new internal borders and to significantly lower levels of permeability at the new external borders.
- Second, Europeanization spurs cross-border cooperation in a multi-facetted process, which includes financial incentives, legal pressures, as in the case of the EU Water Framework directive, and the discursive spread of ideas and paradigms.
- The third aspect is that national governments are losing their role as gatekeepers of transboundary relations (cf. Blatter 2003: 511). What comes to the fore are heterogeneous forms of transboundary governance, including actors from different political-administrative levels and sectors, who are often organised in the form of networks (see fig. 1). These new forms of transboundary relations can be termed

"transnational regionalism" (Schmitt-Egner 1998: 30 f.), "cross-border governance" (Perkmann & Sum 2002: 16) or "para-diplomacy" (Keating 2002: 43 f).

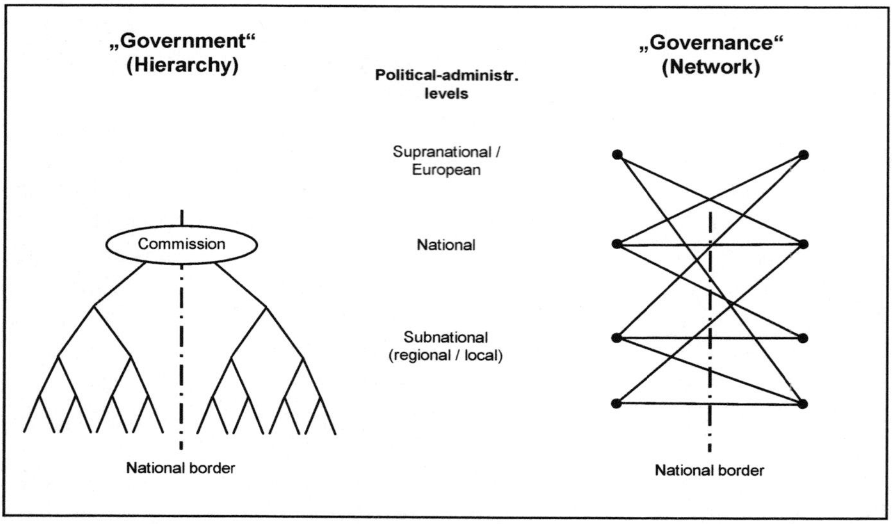

Figure 1. Forms of cross-border interaction patterns: From government to governance (design: M. Leibenath)

- The fourth observation is that borders between sovereign states are no longer the single "Westphalian"[1] line (Brunet-Jailly 2004: 1) separating two countries in all respects. Instead, there is an overlap of different functional spaces which are each delimited individually. What we are currently witnessing is that economic, social, legal, political and identity spaces are to an ever greater extent bounded separately (Christiansen & Jørgensen 2000: 62). This is due to the growing complexity of modern societies and their functional segmentation, which makes it impossible to control all external relations on the basis of one territorial border line (Luhmann 1982: 241).

---

1 The Peace of Westphalia from 1648 officially ended the Thirty Years' War and paved the way towards a mosaic of sovereign, completely autonomous micro-states all across Germany.

3 Sustainable spatial development of border regions in the context of territorial cohesion

A great deal of scholarly work has focused on borders and the development of border regions. Research on borders has even been dubbed a "growth industry" (Bucken-Knapp & Schack 2001: 13) and the growing number of publications on borders has been compared to a "minor avalanche" (Strassoldo & delli Zotti 1982: 1). Most researchers concerned with borders are rooted in the social sciences and have concentrated on issues of identity (e.g. Paasi 1996), social construction of borders (e.g., van Houtum & Strüver 2002) and cross-border institution-building (e.g., Blatter 2001). Furthermore, many researchers, chiefly with economic backgrounds, examine borders as obstacles to flows of goods, capital etc. and seek solutions for overcoming those obstacles (e.g., Huber 2003).

What distinguishes this book from the rest of the "avalanche" is the attempt to bring together contributions from different disciplines under the overall heading of the sustainable development of border regions. It is almost two decades since the Brundtland report (WCED 1987) placed the concept of sustainability on the global political agenda. However, the idea of sustainability as such is much older, dating back to at least the early nineteenth century. Originally, the definition of sustainable development was part of a statement of faith: "Humanity has the ability to make development sustainable – to ensure that it meets the needs of the present without compromising the ability of future generations to meet their own needs" (WCED 1987: 8). The Brundtland report also stressed the concept's dynamic character: "[...] sustainable development is not a fixed state of harmony, but rather a process of change in which the exploitation of resources, the direction of investments, the orientation of technological development, and institutional change are made consistent with future as well as present needs" (WCED 1987: 9). With regard to the breadth of these definitions, one author has noted ironically that "sustainability seeks to provide the best of all possible worlds for people and the environment both now and into the indefinite future" (Wikipedia 2006, no page numbering).

Not surprisingly, the EU has published a very similar, catch-all, visionary definition of sustainable development:

> "Sustainable development offers the European Union a positive long-term vision of a society that is more prosperous and more just, and which promises a cleaner, safer, healthier environment – a society which delivers a better quality of life for us, for our children, and for our grandchildren." (CEC 2001: 2)

Sustainability is a key principle of all EU policies and actions. There are also references to this concept in articles 2 and 6 of the Amsterdam Treaty of 1997 (CEC 2005: 2).

In the European Spatial Development Perspective (ESDP), sustainable development as defined in the Brundtland report is translated into spatial terms as "balanced spatial development. This means, in particular, reconciling the social and economic claims for spatial development with the area's ecological and cultural functions" (EC 1999: 10). The latter statement hints at the often cited three dimensions of sustainable development – economic, social and ecological.

Sustainable and balanced spatial development is closely linked to the notion of territorial cohesion. For instance, the European Commission says in a recent document that "sustainable development seeks to promote a dynamic economy with a high level of [...] social and territorial cohesion and of environmental protection" (CEC 2005: 3). Similarly, the European Conference of Ministers responsible for Regional Planning (CE) mentions as a first principle of planning policy for sustainable development in Europe: "Promoting territorial cohesion through a more balanced social and economic development of regions and improved competitiveness" (CEMAT 2000: 9). However, Gualini (2005: no page numbering) recommends avoiding "an overemphasis on instrumental interpretation of 'territorial cohesion'". It is indeed difficult to find a precise definition of "territorial cohesion". This broad umbrella concept covers the territorial dimension of social and economic cohesion. It refers both to the cohesion of part of a territory to the whole and to the internal cohesiveness within a territory. It aims at reducing existing disparities and avoiding territorial imbalances. It also implies making sectoral policy that has a spatial impact more coherent and encouraging cooperation between regions (EC 2003: 27; Leibenath & Knippschild 2007: 123-125; SUD 2003: 19).

Thus, without running the risk of overstressing the instrumental content of "territorial cohesion", it seems evident that the concept has two core meanings: (a) to avoid spatial imbalances and disparities between regions and (b) to coordinate sectoral policies that have a spatial impact. Both understandings are relevant to the development of European border regions and to research on them. Many border regions are located far from the centres of economic activity. Governments can offer equal access to public services for the inhabitants of these regions only at very high costs. In many cases it can therefore be cost efficient to coordinate the provision of such services across national boundaries. This applies to social and technical infrastructures and services as well as to the development of industrial, commercial or residential sites.

In border regions, horizontal policy coordination across sectors and vertical policy coordination across different levels require particular effort because of the manifold institutional asymmetries still prevailing between countries. Projects whose scope transcends borders need cross-border coordination anyway, as in the case of large transport infrastructure.

Such considerations are also reflected in key documents about sustainable spatial development at the European level. The ESDP lists three types of cross-border planning efforts:

- the preparation of cross-border spatial visions and strategies,
- the regular cross-border fine tuning of all spatially-related planning and measures,
- the setting-up of common cross-border regional plans and land-use plans as the most far-reaching form of cross-border spatial development policy (EC 1999: 44).

In its Guiding Principles for Sustainable Spatial Development, the CEMAT outlines the most important policy sectors with regard to transboundary coordination and planning:

- transport and telecommunications infrastructure and services,
- the conservation and sustainable use of natural resources and water resources,
- public and private services,
- the planning of transfrontier conurbations, cities, and settlement areas of ethnic communities,
- the organisation of transfrontier employment catchment areas,
- pollution (CEMAT 2000: 17).

Cross-sectoral coordination of spatially relevant policy and the preparation of spatial plans and visions belong to the day-to-day business of planners. These are also common subjects of research on spatial development. What is special about doing this in a transboundary context? And what are specific challenges for research on sustainable transboundary spatial development?

4 Addressing border-related gaps

The present volume is organised in four main sections. The first one focuses on the effects of external influences and framework conditions on cross-border governance. Miosga highlights the implications of spatial development policies at the European and national levels with special focus on Germany. He concentrates on the revised structure of European regional policy and on the new German guiding principles for spatial development. Ciok and Raczyk show how one piece of European regional policy, namely strand A of the Community Initiative INTERREG III was implemented on the Polish-German Border. They scrutinize the scope and character of cooperation as well as the compliance of particular projects with the principles of the European Union and national policies.

The second section of the book examines cross-border governance at the regional level and includes case studies from the Dutch-Belgian border and the Austrian-German border. The chief interest is on institutions and institutional capacity-building, but also on interdepencies between different levels of policy-making. De Vries looks at cross-border cooperation in the Rhine-Scheldt Delta. He discusses the extent of governmental integration across borders in this Dutch-Belgian border region and analyses governance structures and policies concerning the physical environment. Deppisch takes the Austrian-German Euregio 'Via Salina' as a case to study social capital and other main influences on governance processes in cross-border micro-regions. She is also concerned with the effects of European institutions and asks to what extent such regions are nothing but a response to INTERREG or whether they are the expression of a pro-active approach.

The third section features cross-border cooperation between cities and metropolitan regions. Jaššo begins with an analysis of cross-border cooperation challenges in the Vienna-Bratislava Region, which shares a joint history but is currently characterised by pronounced imbalances. He introduces three scenarios of how this transboundary region could develop and evaluates their estimated implications. Knippschild presents two case studies of cross-border, interurban cooperation between smaller cities in the Polish-Czech-German triangle. His aim is to outline the preconditions for inter-urban cooperation in this particular geographic area and to identify the major factors influencing cross-border cooperation. Korcelli-Olejniczak takes us back to the metropolitan level and analyses functional complementarity as a basis for inter-metropolitan collaboration and networking, based on a case-study on cultural activities in Berlin and Warsaw. She perceives culture as an aspect of transboundary development problems and seeks potential for inter-urban co-operation and networking within this field.

The fourth section is dedicated to selected sectoral perspectives on border regions, i.e., transport, nature conservation, the environment, and the economy. In his article, Kormornicki documents the transformations that have taken place in the domain of transport infrastructure and cross-border traffic on 'new' (since 2004) internal and external boundaries of the European Union. In the first case, the example of the Polish-German border is considered, while in the second case the example of the Polish-Ukrainian border is presented. Nolte describes and analyses the situation of two transboundary biosphere reserve regions in Hungary, Slovakia, the Czech Republic, and Germany. Degórski discusses the environmental dimension of transboundary spatial development and stresses the importance of natural resources for the development of border areas. He examines whether the natural environment can constitute a driving force for the emergence of coherent border regions. Dołata takes the case of a special economic zone inside Poland, but close to the German border, as a starting point for exploring the role of such zones in the development of Poland's border regions.

The book concludes with an article by Leibenath, Korcelli-Olejniczak & Knippschild in which they summarize and compare the main findings of the individual chapters. Furthermore, they identify perspectives for further research which could contribute to bridging or eventually closing the persisting gaps in knowledge on cross-border governance and sustainable spatial development in Central Europe.

References

Blatter J (2001) Debordering the World of States: Towards a Multi-level System in Europe and a Multi-Polity System in North America? Insights from Border Regions. European Journal of International Relations 7(2), 175–209

Blatter J (2003) Beyond Hierarchies and Networks: Institutional Logics and Change in Trans-boundary Political Spaces during the 20th century. Governance: An International Journal of Policy, Administration and Institution 16(4), 503–526

Brunet-Jailly E (2004) Toward a Model of Border Studies: What Do We Learn from the Study of the Canadian-American Border? Journal of Borderlands Studies 19(1), 1–12

Bucken-Knapp G, Schack M (2001) Borders Matter, But How? In: Bucken-Knapp G, Schack M (eds) Borders Matter: Transboundary Regions in Contemporary Europe. Institut for Graenseregionsforskning, Aabenraa: 13–28

CEC (= Commission of the European Communities) (2001) Communication from the Commission. A Sustainable Europe for a Better World: A European Union Strategy for Sustainable Development. Available online: http://europa.eu.int/eur-lex/en/com/cnc/2001/com2001_0264en01.pdf, 10.04.2006

CEC (= Commission of the European Communities) (2005) Communication from the Commission to the Council and the European Parliament. Draft Declaration on Guiding Principles for Sustainable Development. Available online: http://europa.eu.int/comm/sustainable/docs/COM_2005_0218_F_EN_ACTE.pdf, 10.04.2006

CEMAT (=European Conference of Ministers responsible for Regional Planning) (2000) Guiding Principles for Sustainable Spatial Development of the

European Continent. Available online: http://www.coe.int/t/e/cultural_co-operation/environment/cemat/GPSSDEC/Principles.pdf?L=E, 10.04.2006

Christiansen T & Jørgensen KE (2000), Transnational Governance 'above' and 'below' the State: The Changing Nature of Borders in the New Europe. Regional and Federal Studies 10, 62–77

EC (= European Commission) (1999), ESDP. European Spatial Development Perspective. Towards Balanced and Sustainable Development of the Territory of the European Union. Available online: http://europa.eu.int/comm/regional_policy/sources/docoffic/official/reports/pdf/sum_en.pdf, 10.04.2006

EC (= European Commission) (2003), A new partnership for cohesion. Convergence – Competitiveness – Cooperation. Third report on economic and social cohesion. Available online: http://europa.eu.int/comm/regional_policy/sources/docoffic/official/reports/cohesion3/cohesion3_en.htm, 12.04.2006

Gualini E (2005) Europeanization and Governance Rescaling: "Territorial Cohesion" as Opportunity for "Re-politicizing" European Spatial Policy and Planning? Available online: http://aesop2005.scix.net/cgi-bin/papers/Show?_id=340, 19.08.2005

Huber P (2003) On the Determinants of Cross-border Cooperation of Austrian Firms with Central and Eastern European Partners. Regional Studies 37.9, 957–955

Keating M (2002) Paradiplomatie und regionale Netzwerke [= Para-Diplomacy and Regional Networks]. In: Europäisches Zentrum für Föderalismus-Forschung (ed) Jahrbuch des Föderalismus 2002. Nomos, Baden-Baden, 43–53

Leibenath M, Knippschild R (2007) Territorial Cohesion and Transboundary Governance: insights from the Polish-German and the Czech-German Borders. In: Scholich D (ed) German Annual of Spatial Research and Policy 2007. Territorial Cohesion. Springer, Berlin, Heidelberg, 123–150

Luhmann N (1982) Territorial Borders as System Boundaries. In: Strassoldo R, delli Zotti G (eds) Cooperation and Conflict in Border Areas. Franco Angeli Editore, Milano, 235–244

Paasi A (1996) Inclusion, exclusion and territorial identities – the meanings of boundaries in the globalizing geopolitical landscape. Nordisk Samhällsgeografisk Tidskrift. Available online: http://www.geo.ruc.dk/nst/paasi23.html, 13.03.2006

Perkmann M & Sum N-L (2002) Globalization, Regionalization and Cross-Border Regions: Scales, Discourses and Governance. In Perkmann M, Sum N-L (eds.) Globalization, Regionalization, and Cross-Border Regions. Macmillan, Basingstoke, 3–24

Schindegger F, Tatzberger G & Illés I (2005) ESPON project 1.1.3, Enlargement of the European Union and the wider European Perspective as regards its Polycentric Spatial Structure Part 3, Annexes A-E, Annex C, Symmetries and Asymmetries of Border Regions in the new member states and enlargement area. Available online: http://www.espon.lu/online/documentation/projects/thematic/3710/fr_1.1.3_part3_051231_annex-c_f1.pdf, 17.04.2006

Schmitt-Egner P (1998) 'Grenzüberschreitende Zusammenarbeit' (GZA) in Europa als Gegenstand wissenschaftlicher Forschung und Strategie transnationaler Praxis. Anmerkungen zur Theorie, Empirie und Praxis des Transnationalen Regionalismus. In: Brunn G & Schmitt-Egner P (eds) Grenzüberschreitende Zusammenarbeit in Europa. Theorie – Empirie – Praxis. Baden-Baden: Nomos, 27–77

Strassoldo R, delli Zotti G (eds) (1982) Cooperation and Conflict in Border Areas. Franco Angeli Editore, Milano

SUD (= EU Working Group on Spatial and Urban Development) (2003) Managing the Territorial Dimension of EU Policies after Enlargement. Available online: http://europa.eu.int/comm/regional_policy/debate/document/futur/member/esdp.pdf, 12.04.2006

Van Houtum H, Strüver A (2002) Borders, Strangers, Doors and Bridges. Space & Polity 6(2), 141-146

WCED (= World Commission on Environment and Development) (1987) Our Common Future. Oxford: Oxford University Press

Wikipedia (2006) Sustainability. Available online: http://en.wikipedia.org/wiki/Sustainability, 10.04.2006

I External influences and framework conditions

Implications of spatial development policies at European and national levels for border regions
The case of Germany

Manfred Miosga

Identity & Image Coaching AG, Weßling, Germany

1 Border regions and sustainable regional development

Border regions have always been of particular importance for the integration of the European Union. They are the interfaces between people of different nationalities with different cultures and languages. The success of the integration process can be measured by the extent to which frontiers lose their significance in the everyday life of people living in border regions. Hence, promoting cross-border cooperation is one of the most fundamental approaches in European regional policy to make the integration process irreversible. Furthermore, cross-border cooperation plays an important role in preparing the accession of new Member States.

A border region is a certain type of region with specific problems. Within each country, many – though not all – border regions suffer from various handicaps: located at the outer boundaries of the country, their economic structure and infrastructural endowment are frequently weak, they are often sparsely populated and affected by out-migration, and located far from the centres of political decision-making. This makes them eligible for many EU and national regional development programmes.

This paper looks at the intensive current discussion on the need for changes and a reorientation of objective in two policy fields of high relevance for the sustainable development of border regions. The new architecture of European regional policy and its funding tools are addressed.

This is important for border regions because initiatives for cross-border cooperation are mainly funded through the former Community Initiative INTERREG III A as a part of European regional policy. German spatial development and planning policy and the new national guiding principles for spatial development are examined. However, the bottom line of these two discussions is similar and points in the same direction. In both policy fields a new orientation towards a growth paradigm is apparent. The concrete consequences of this reorientation on the sustainable development of border regions is discussed at the end of this contribution.

2 The revision of European regional policy

2.1 The Lisbon-Agenda as overarching guideline for European policies

European regional policy is based on article 158 of the Treaty establishing the European Community. This article commissions the community to stimulate harmonious development, to support less-developed regions in catching-up to the level of the community and thus to strengthen territorial cohesion. This clearly formulates the idea of balanced territorial development and sets the main focus on reducing disparities between regions.

After a long process of consultation, the European Council decided in October 2006 on the new Community strategic guidelines for cohesion policy in the 2007–2013 programming period (OJ 2006/L 291/11). With this decision, a final point was marked for revising the whole system of European regional policy. This revision had become enlargement of the EU and the significant efforts required to integrate the new EU Member States in Eastern and Central Europe into the Community, and to ensure the social and territorial cohesion of the EU-25. On the other hand, the discussion was fuelled by the continuing weakness of the Communities' economy since the 1990s on a global scale, and the need to strengthen economic growth in the Union.

Owing to globalisation and intensified competition of the world's main economic blocks, such as North America, South-East Asia, China and Europe, the position of the EU with regard to productivity, innovation and employment risks deteriorating. In order to cope with these challenges, the European Council adopted the Lisbon Agenda, which set a new strategic goal for the Union for the coming decade: "to become the most competitive and dynamic knowledge-based economy in the world" (OJ 2006/L 210/19).

The main objectives of the Lisbon strategy are:

- to increase the overall employment level to close to 70% by 2010, which is considered to be full employment;
- to increase economic productivity and innovativeness to match the best in the world;
- to accept the challenge of an information society, as a digital, knowledge-based economy and to facilitate access for businesses and the public to an inexpensive world-class communications infrastructure;
- to establish a European area of research and innovation;
- to create a favourable environment for starting up and developing innovative businesses, especially small and medium enterprises (SMEs);
- to complete the internal market through economic reform and further liberalisation;
- to consolidate public finances;
- to modernise the European social model and to adapt social protection.

Member States have to translate the Lisbon Agenda as an overall strategy into national and regional policy which is evaluated periodically at the European level.

At the summit meeting in February 2005, the European Council again argued for a new partnership for growth and jobs as a means of reviving the Lisbon strategy. Subsequently all community policies were oriented towards meeting the objectives of the Lisbon strategy. This explicitly concerned European regional policy and the organisation of European structural funds. The presidency of the European Council concluded in March 2005: "To achieve these objectives, the Union must mobilise all appropriate national and Community resources – including the cohesion policy" (European Commission 2005a).

This implies that cohesion policy must aim not only to integrate the new Member States and reduce disparities between regions but also help improve the global competitiveness of the EU as a whole (European Commission 2004a). Thus, greater emphasis will be placed on the growth-oriented component of European regional policy in addition and partly in contradiction to the aim of balancing regional development.

To this end, the European Commission initiated discussion in 2001 on the future of cohesion policy and the application of structural funds. In July 2004, the European Commission passed its suggestions on the redefinition of objectives and the eligibility of regions (European Commission 2004b).

2.2 The new strategic guidelines on economic, social and territorial cohesion

In the further process and after a number of consultations, the European Commission submitted a new concept for the cohesion policy in July 2005, consisting of a new of strategic orientation model, the upgrading of the role of the cities within cohesion policy and a revision of the eligibility of regions in the enlarged Union. The strategic guidelines have been decided even by the European Council (OJ 2006/L 291/11) to underline their importance and to enhance their legitimacy.

The new strategic guidelines are designed to integrate the Lisbon objectives into cohesion policy under three priorities: (a) the shift to a knowledge-based economy, (b) investment in infrastructure and environment protection, as well as creation of more and better jobs, and (c) territorial cooperation (see table 1).

2.3 The new EU cohesion policy

In addition to the new strategic guidelines, new regulations about the objectives and the eligibility of regions are part of the new architecture of EU cohesion policy. The three priority structural fund objectives for the period 2000 to 2006 – Objective 1: regions lagging behind in development; Objective 2: regions undergoing economic and social conversion; Objective 3: training systems and employment promotion – have been replaced for the 2007 to 2013 period by a new set: (a) convergence, (b) regional competitiveness and employment, and (c) territorial cooperation (DG-Regio 2004).

2.3.1 The new 'convergence' objective

Very much in line with Objective 1 of the 2000–2006 programming period, the purpose of the convergence objective is to speed up economic convergence of less-developed regions. This is to be achieved by

- improving conditions for growth and employment,
- investment in human and physical capital,
- innovation and the development of the knowledge society,
- encouraging adaptability to economic and social change
- environmental protection, and
- improving administrative efficiency.

First and foremost, the convergence objective addresses regions whose per capita gross domestic product (GDP) is less than 75% of the average for the enlarged EU, calculated on the figures available for the three years prior to adopting the regulation. This is mainly the case for the majority of new Member States.

Table 1. Guidelines and priorities of Community strategic guidelines on cohesion

Sectoral Guidelines	Priorities
1. Making Europe and its regions more attractive places in which to invest and work	1.1 Expanding and improving infrastructure 1.2 Strengthening synergies between environmental protection and growth 1.3 Addressing Europe's intensive use of traditional energy sources
2. Improving knowledge and innovation for growth	2.1 Increasing and better targeting investment in RTD 2.2 Facilitating innovation and promoting entrepreneurship 2.3 Promoting the information society for all 2.4 Improving access to finance
3. More and better Jobs	3.1 Attracting and retaining more people in employment and modernising social protection systems 3.2 Improving the adaptability of workers and enterprises and labour market flexibility 3.3 Increasing investment in human capital through better education and skills 3.4 Administrative capacity 3.5 Helping maintain a healthy labour force
Territorial Dimension of cohesion Policy	**Fields of action**
a) The contribution of cities to growth and jobs	- Improving competitiveness in urban areas - Rehabilitating the physical infrastructure - Promoting entrepreneurship, local employment and community development - Strengthening integration and security, fighting discrimination
b) Rural areas, fisheries and peripheries	- Supporting economic diversification - Ensuring minimum access to services of general economic interest - Developing and integrated approach to tourism and promoting development poles
c) Cooperation	- Cross-border cooperation - Transnational cooperation - Interregional cooperation - Focusing on growth and jobs - Contributing to economic and social integration - Improving transport and communication infrastructure

Source: own compilation based on the Council Decision of 6.10.2006 (OJ 2006/L 291/11)

In addition, a 'phasing out' support will be granted, on a decreasing basis, for the former Objective 1 regions whose per capita GDP exceeds the 75% limit due solely to the statistical effects of enlargement.

60% of expenditure for the convergence regions is to be earmarked for activities contributing to the Lisbon Agenda.

2.3.2 The new 'regional competitiveness and employment' objective

For the rest of the Union, a twofold approach is proposed. On the one hand, the regional development programmes in the frame of the European Regional Development Fund (ERDF) are intended to strengthen regional competitiveness and attractiveness. On the other hand, programmes at the national or appropriate territorial level financed by the European Social Fund (ESF) are to help workers and companies, on the basis of the European employment strategy, to adapt to change and encourage the development of job markets that award priority to social inclusion.

All regions are eligible for this objective, provided they are not covered by the convergence objective. It is up to Member States to specify the regions for which they submit a programme regarding this objective. The Community zoning of the former Objective 2 thus no longer applies.

Regions under the former Objective 1 that are no longer eligible under the convergence objective due to their economic achievements will receive specific 'phasing out' support on a decreasing basis until 2013 to consolidate the process of catching up. The share of Lisbon-related activities is to be 75% of all expenditure.

2.3.3 The 'European territorial cooperation' objective

The purpose of this new objective is inspired by the experience of the Community Initiative INTERREG and is to strengthen cooperation at three levels:

- cross-border cooperation,
- cooperation between transnational zones and
- networks for cooperation and the exchange of experiences throughout the Union.

The cooperation objective thus seeks to encourage balanced, harmonious and sustainable development throughout the European area.

The 'cross-border cooperation' strand covers regions lying along internal land borders and certain external land borders (see fig. 1). It also contributes to the cross-border components of the 'European neighbourhood and partnership instrument' and the 'Instrument for pre-accession'. The whole EU territory is eligible for the financing of European cooperation and exchange networks. The territorial cooperation objective is to replace the former Community Initiative INTERREG.

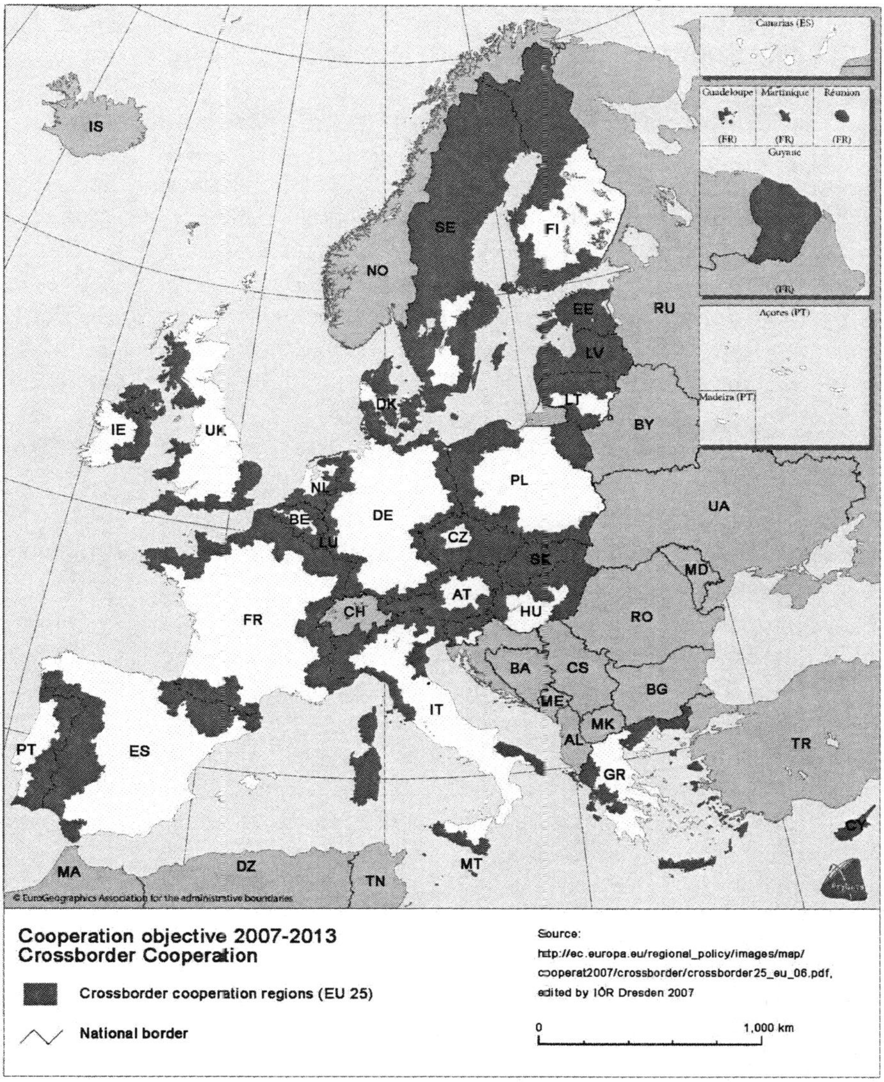

Figure 1. Co-operation objective 2007-2013 – Cross-border cooperation

3 New perspectives for spatial development policy in Germany

3.1 Requirements for adjustment and modernization

Consonant to the debate on reform of the European cohesion policy, the need to adjust the main principles of spatial development policy in Germany has been intensively discussed. Parallel to revision of the Federal Regional Planning Act in 1998, discussion arose on new perspectives for spatial development. New guiding principles are to facilitate reaction to changing framework conditions and new challenges. They include:

- increasing regional disparities in Germany, in particular between eastern and the western Germany,
- worsening demographic changes,
- intensified competition at the European and global levels,
- development towards a knowledge-based economy,
- different understanding of the government's role in spatial development,
- an ongoing crisis of public finance,
- and, last but not least, European integration, which requires account to be taken of the European dimensions of spatial development.

More in-depth consideration of spatial structural changes also reveals large-scale polarisation tendencies, as well as an increasing heterogeneity at different spatial levels. "Subspaces are no longer converging; the differences between them are now growing" (Aring 2005: 41, translation by the author). This requires a more differentiated approach to spatial development than in times of economic prosperity.

3.2 New guiding principles and political orientations

The 2000 and 2005 spatial development reports (BBR 2000; BBR 2005a) confirmed these changes and challenges in more fundamental analyses. The need to reorient spatial development policy was evident and led to the establishment of a task force and a formal commission by the Ministerial Committee on Spatial Planning, MKRO (2004)[2].

Since September 2005, the results have been available in the form of a detailed discussion paper (BBR 2005b). The MKRO passed the new guide-

[2] The responsibility for spatial development and planning in Germany is shared between the federal government and the governments of the 16 states. The MKRO committee comprises the ministers responsible for spatial planning in the federal and state governments.

lines in a shortened and revised version in June 2006 after a period of intense debate (MKRO 2006).

Three new guiding principles are suggested:

1. promoting economic growth and development,
2. securing and adjusting the supply of basic services of public interest, and
3. managing land use.

The first guideline is a commitment to promote economic growth and innovation. In order to promote growth, economic centres and innovation networks are to be supported and fostered. To avoid isolating peripheral regions, "an area of mutual responsibility" is to be provided for to encourage cooperation between metropolitan regions and other urban centres and with peripheral regions.

The provision of public infrastructure and services increasingly depends on economic considerations, especially in less densely populated areas affected by out-migration. Under these circumstances, it is hard to image how the existing polycentric network of cities can be maintained at its current density. However, minimum standards of service are to be defined (BBR 2005b: 21 f.).

The new German spatial development policy marks an elementary shift. "From the point of view of spatial planning, the primary objective of economic development is not to reduce disparities, but to contribute equally to promoting growth and a knowledge-based economy" (BBR 2005: 23, translation by the author). This perspective defines metropolitan growth areas as an important approach, but the ultimate aim is to 'strengthen strengths' on a broad front" (BBR 2005: 24, translation by the author). The position of German cities and regions as a whole in European competition is to be improved.

4 Comments on the new orientation of European and German spatial development policies

4.1 Dominance of the economic growth paradigm

Both the new European cohesion policy and Germany's new spatial development policy consonantly emphasize the promotion of economic growth as an overarching objective.

For the European Commission, it is essential to concentrate resources in areas that accelerate structural transformation towards a knowledge-based economy. Convergent development in the Community is to be achieved by stimulating specific growth potentials rather than through transfer payments. The capacity to cope with structural transformation is to be increased in particular by investment in innovative sectors of the economy and R&D activities. Acceleration of the transformation process towards a knowledge-based economy is also a major goal of the new German spatial development policy.

According to the competition-oriented approach of the Lisbon Agenda with its focuses on deregulation, flexible labour markets and cuts in welfare payments (Bischoff & Detje 2007: 18), the conceptual shift in regional development policy aims to strengthen regional competitiveness. This may lead to increased polarization between regions and is in contradiction with the traditional objectives of promoting harmonious, balanced and sustainable spatial development, of reducing regional disparities and providing comparable living conditions.

This "watershed" (DG-Regio 2004) in the regional policy towards growth orientation is justified by the need to meet the Lisbon targets. In this regard "all regions – especially those where the potential for higher productivity and employment is greatest – have their part to play" (European Commission 2005a: 6). This also implies that stronger regions are to receive support for tapping their potentials. But this could widen the gap between stronger and weaker regions, as the latter have a worse starting position for creating growth and coping with the challenge of the knowledge economy.

On the other hand, the European Commission stresses that already "by mobilising the potential for growth that exists in all regions, cohesion policy improves the geographical balance of economic development and raises the potential rate of growth in the Union as a whole" (European Commission 2005a: 6). For lagging regions this may sound euphemistic.

Similarly, spatial planning policy in Germany is currently undergoing a fundamental shift – away from the objective of creating equivalent living standards in all regions. Strengthening the strength of all regions consequently means that – with regard to spatial structure – metropolitan areas that are already strong will be further supported to boost overall economic growth. Spatial planning is supposed to contribute to improving their growth potential, for example by concentrating metropolitan functions and by improving land-use patterns and transport systems. The cities and regions beyond the metropolitan commuter belt are left to improve their competitiveness and growth potential on their own.

With regard to the situation in peripheral regions affected by economic decline and out-migration, federal spatial planning policy seems to have resigned and given up the struggle for a slowdown or even a reversal of the negative trend. Therefore, the perspective "securing and adjusting services of public interest" includes a concept for dismantling infrastructure facilities in weaker regions. This is to be undertaken on the basis of newly defined minimum standards for supply and the accessibility of supply facilities, which are also to legitimate the abandonment of established standards while helping to avoid the permanent downgrading of standards. The polycentric network of cities and the principle of decentralized concentration remain important. However, the new policy implies a tolerable deconstruction of this concept: a reduction in the number of higher-level central places and thus a less dense network of public services supply in rural areas. This might be acceptable in the event of improved accessibility in metropolitan regions, increased mobility, and mobile and more flexible forms of public service supply. Nevertheless, this also represents a "watershed" in national spatial development policy – for both financial and conceptual reasons.

4.2 The specific contribution of cities and the risk of spatial polarization

In both European and German spatial development policy, cities play an important role because urban agglomerations are usually growth poles of the knowledge-based economy. They provide the "critical mass" of firms and institutions that are needed to establish technology clusters and SME-networks. That is why the European Commissioner in charge of regional policy presented a working paper on "Cohesion Policy and cities: the urban contribution to growth and jobs in the regions" at an informal meeting of ministers responsible for urban policy in December 2005. The paper initiated a consultation process with the aim of amplifying and complemented Community Strategic Guidelines by elaborating and strengthening the urban dimension.

The Commission considers cities and the metropolitan areas to be the most important partners for growth oriented policy. While cities and metropolitan areas are the basis of economic development, they are also the locus of major obstacles to higher growth and more jobs – notably social exclusion and environmental degradation. "The effort for growth and jobs within a context of global competition needs to build on the resources of urban areas, regardless of size." (European Commission 2005b: 4).

However, cities are not regarded as isolated actors but in the context of their surrounding rural areas, as there are several functional linkages. The "urban component requires national and regional governments to make strategic choices in identifying and strengthening growth poles" (European

Commission 2005b: 3). From the European Commission's viewpoint, these poles serve wider territories and contribute to the sustainable and balanced development of the territory as a whole.

In the context of the Lisbon strategy, cities are outstandingly important because they provide the essential functions for a competitive, knowledge-based economy. This requires concentration on industries and sectors in which ideas, innovation and technology have a large share of value added. Cities and growth poles must intensify their efforts to create infrastructural conditions for the development of a knowledge-based economy and to create an attractive environment for knowledge workers. This includes raising the general educational level and providing efficient educational systems. Such conditions, however, cannot be provided in all cities at the same standard.

By clearly putting the focus on the knowledge economy and the employee requirements – the "high-potentials" – and with its commitment to strengthening growth poles, European regional policy abandons the principle of extensive support throughout a larger territory. Thus, the existing trend in favour of agglomerations and cities is consciously and systematically reinforced: structural change towards a knowledge-based economy is a dynamic process that depends strongly on positive agglomeration effects and which leads to a concentration of R&D functions, technology-based SMEs, and innovative start-ups in urban agglomerations (Frey & Zimmermann 2005).

The Lisbon-Agenda calls on the EU and Member States to make a serious effort to open their markets to service industries and to strengthen their competitiveness by promoting research, technological development and innovation and by investing in transport infrastructure, universities and ICT-infrastructure. This again will favour regions that are already well endowed with functions and components beneficial for a knowledge-based economy.

Thus, the new European policy following the Lisbon strategy is subsequently intensifying the tendency towards spatial disparities at different levels. The highly modernized metropolitan areas of the European Union along the "Blue Banana" or inside the so-called "European Pentagon" which is delimited by London, Paris, Milan, Munich, and Hamburg will benefit from structural change anyway. Here, the main R&D facilities and the most productive industries are concentrated, the level of infrastructure and the service quality is highest and expenditure on future-oriented research and industries is greatest. The big capitals and metropolitan areas of countries on the margins of the EU such as Madrid, Rome, Athens, the Scandinavian agglomerations, Prague, Budapest, and Warsaw might play a role.

But inside the less developed countries and particularly in Central and Eastern European countries, increasing polarisation between metropolitan and peripheral areas will be the consequence. Moreover, accelerating structural transformation will reinforce push and pull factors for migration, as indicated by persistently high immigration rates to Europe's economic centres. Migrants are mostly enterprising, well educated, young and mobile. Vice versa, this implies a brain-drain from peripheral regions of the EU.

5 Consequences for border regions

5.1 Cross-border cooperation remains an important part of regional development policy

With regard to border regions, support for cross-border cooperation plays an important role in the new programming period 2007–2013 for European cohesion policy. The new German perspectives for spatial development also indicate that cross-border cooperation is an important means for strengthening the international aspects of spatial planning policy (MKRO 2006: 9 f.).

One of the three objectives of the new cohesion policy, territorial cooperation remains important, substantially valorising cross-border collaboration in border regions. Promoting cross-border cooperation will help to mitigate the obstacles created by borders and to catch-up to the level of other regions.

To facilitate cross-border cooperation and overcome legal difficulties between Member States in regulating cross-border cooperation, a special new legal entity has been created: "European grouping of territorial cooperation". This formal instrument is designed to facilitate cross-border cooperation by implementing relevant projects, whether or not co-financed by the Community (2006/L 210/19).

Nevertheless, the Commission expects cross-border cooperation to be promoted by strengthening the competitiveness of the region. Cooperation programmes are to be tailored to fit the particular situation in each border region. However, the Commission insists that the main priorities – economic growth and the creation of new jobs – be met. As a pre-condition for establishing or developing cross-border contacts, the Commission proposes improving the transport and communication infrastructure and, where necessary, developing new connections. Where the basic conditions for cross-border cooperation are already in place, resources are to be concentrated on activities like innovation, research and development, the promotion of cross-border labour market integration, cross-border water management and flood control (European Commission 2005a: 36). Thus cross-border cooperation is expected to contribute to the Lisbon Agenda.

The up-grading of European cooperation activities led the Commission in 2005 to propose a substantially increased budget of € 13.2 bn for the new third objective – more than twice as much as in the former INTERREG III budget (Hübner 2005). However, a closer look at the figures of the Council agreement on the budget 2007–2013, shows that the budget was significantly cut to about half of what the Commission had initially proposed. The final budget roughly equals that of the former Community Initiative INTERREG III. For cross-border initiatives in border regions – the former strand A of INTERREG – 77% of the overall budget for objective three is now earmarked. But the reduction of the budget for objective three reduced resources for cross-border cooperation in absolute terms: from the original € 6.3 billion suggested by the Commission to € 5.77 billion (Council of the European Union 2005).

The length of internal and external EU borders has increased significantly due to EU enlargement in 2004 and 2007. Moreover, maritime borders are now eligible for funding, as well. This means that the average amount of money available per cross-border region has clearly been reduced (Helander 2005).

5.2 Sustainable development of border regions?

The resources earmarked for the cross-border component of objective three are to be allocated among the Member States "…on the basis of the population of the NUTS level III regions in terrestrial and maritime border areas, as a share of the total population of all the eligible regions" (Council of the European Union 2005: 13). This allocation scheme favours border regions with high growth potential, which are usually much more densely populated and therefore receive a greater share of support. This is in line with the Lisbon strategy. But in terms of a balanced regional development, including support for lagging regions, this allocation of funds has to be questioned.

As spatial development policy in Germany and the whole policy of the European Union are directed more and more towards growth, a concentration of development in metropolitan growth areas can be expected. Peripheral regions are increasingly regarded in terms of their relation with metropolitan areas functional dependence and orientation on urban agglomerations.

Instead of promoting the self-reliance of peripheral and rural areas, they are treated as functionally supplementing metropolitan areas.

Regional policy will lose its character as tool for redistributing resources. Lagging and peripheral regions will be increasingly left to their own devices, to self-initiative and self-help. The policy of supporting growth potentials privileges the existing growth poles of the European Union. This tends to reinforce regional disparities and therefore runs contrary to efforts to raise the standard of living in the new EU Member States to the level of the former EU-15. There are relatively few urban agglomerations in the new Member States that can compete with the metropolitan growth areas of western European, e.g., Warsaw, Prague, Budapest and the Bratislava-Vienna metropolitan region. This will most likely reinforce monocentric and polarised structures in Central and Eastern Europe.

The consequences for border regions are quite differentiated: border regions in Western Europe will generally benefit from the strengthening of established growth poles such as the "Blue Banana" or the "Pentagon". Cross-border cooperation in the sense of sustainable development faces the well-known challenges arising from suburban growth in metropolitan regions: protection of open spaces, controlling the urbanisation process, resource-efficient transport management, and assurance of intraregional accessibility. These challenges make cross-border cooperation in spatial planning essential.

The strengthening of growth areas implies the danger of an aggravation of social and spatial disparities in the EU. A growing number of "losers of integration" will boost centrifugal forces in the Community. However, border regions are the interfaces of European Integration. The more cross-border networks can strengthen, the less vulnerable to disruption these interfaces will be. Cross-border cooperation, different smaller and larger projects of economic, social and cultural cooperation can significantly contribute to attaining this goal. German experience is that cross-border relationships were important in reconstructing bridges and links after World War II. It has also played a major role in the establishment and evolution of the EU. Bearing this in mind, everyday cross-border cooperation in border regions is becoming increasingly important for European cohesion – in particular under the terms of a selective growth policy in Europe.

References

Aring J (2005) Modernisierung der Raumordnung. Impulsstatement zur Arbeitsgruppe 1: Zwischen 'dezentraler Konzentration' und Metropolenförderung [Modernization of Spatial Planning. Presentation in Working Group 1: Between 'de-centralized concentration and support for metropolitan regions]. In: Institut für Landes- und Stadtentwicklungsforschung und Bauwesen des Landes Nordrhein-Westfalen (ed) Ausgleich versus Wachstum – Paradigmenwechsel in der räumlichen Planung? 10. Konferenz für Planerinnen und Planer NRW. Dokumentation [Balance versus Growth – Paradigm Change in Spatial Planning? 10th Conference of Planners from North Rhine-Westphalia. Documentation]. ILS, Gelsenkirchen, 39–49

BBR (= Bundesamt für Bauwesen und Raumordnung) (2000) Raumordnungsbericht 2000 [Spatial Development Report 2000]. BBR, Bonn

BBR (= Bundesamt für Bauwesen und Raumordnung) (2005a) Raumordnungsbericht 2005 [Spatial Development Report 2005]. BBR, Bonn

BBR (= Bundesamt für Bauwesen und Raumordnung) (2005b) Leitbilder und Handlungsstrategien für die Raumentwicklung in Deutschland. Diskussionspapier [Visions and Strategies for Spatial Development in Germany. Discussion Paper]. Available online: http://www.bbr.bund.de/raumordnung/raumentwicklung/download/Diskussionspapier_2005-09-01.pdf, visited on 28.03.2006

Bischoff J, Detje R (2007) Das Europäische Sozialmodell und die Gewerkschaften [The European Social Model and the Trade Unions]. Supplement to the journal Sozialismus 1.2007

Council of the European Union (2005) Financial Perspective 2007-2013. Available online: http://ue.eu.int/ueDocs/cms_Data/docs/pressData/en/misc/87677.pdf, visited on 28.03.2006

DG-Regio (European Commission, Directorate-General for Regional Policy) (2004) Inforegio. Factsheet. Cohesion policy: the 2007 watershed. Legislative proposals by the European Commission for the reform of cohesion policy (2007-13 period). Available online: http://europa.eu.int/comm/regional_policy/sources/docgener/informat/reg2007_en.pdf, visited on 28.03.2006

European Commission (2004a) A new partnership for cohesion. Convergence, Competitiveness, Cooperation. Third report on economic and social cohesion. Available online: http://europa.eu.int/comm/regional_policy/sources/docoffic/official/reports/cohesion3/cohesion3_en.htm, visited on 28.03.2006

European Commission (2004b) Proposal of 14 July 2004 for a Council Regulation laying down general provisions on the European Regional Development Fund, the European Social Fund and the Cohesion Fund. Available online: http://europa.eu.int/scadplus/leg/en/lvb/g24231.htm, visited on 28.03.2006

European Commission (2005a) Cohesion Policy in Support of Growth and Jobs: Community Strategic Guidelines, 2007-2013. Available online: http://europa.eu.int/comm/regional_policy/sources/docoffic/2007/osc/050706osc_en.pdf, visited on 30.03.2006

European Commission (2005b) Cohesion Policy and cities: the urban contribution to growth and jobs in the regions. Available online: http://europa.eu.int/comm/regional_policy/consultation/urban/contri_urban_en.pdf, visited on 29.03.2006

Frey R, Zimmermann H (2005) Neue Rahmenbedingungen für die Raumordnung als Chance für marktwirtschaftliche Instrumente [New Framework Conditions for Spatial Planning as an Opportunity for Market-based Instruments]. DISP 161, 5-18. Available online: http://www.nsl.ethz.ch/index.php/content/download/1100/6759/file/, visited on 1 March 2007

Helander E (2005) Start up of programming for Objective 3. Power-point-presentation on the INTERACT conference 'Steps towards Territorial Co-Operation Programmes 2007-2013' Brussels, 28 September 2005. Available online: http://www.interact-eu.net/download/application/pdf/879839, visited on 30.03.2006

Hübner D (2005) Speech on the agreement on the budget for cohesion policy in the financial perspectives 2007–2013 at the REGI Committee. Available online: http://europa.eu.int/rapid/pressReleasesAction.do?reference=SPEECH/05/753&format=HTML&aged=1&language=EN&guiLanguage=fr, visited on 28.03.2006

MKRO (= Geschäftsstelle der Ministerkonferenz für Raumordnung im Bundesministerium für Verkehr, Bau und Stadtentwicklung) (2004) Beschluss der MKRO zur Aufstellung neuer Leitbilder und Handlungsstrategien für die Raumentwicklung in Deutschland, in: MKRO (ed.) (2006), Leitbilder und Handlungsstrategien für die Raumentwicklung in Deutschland [Visions and Strategies for Spatial Development in Germany]. Available online: http://www.bmvbs.de/Anlage/original_982048/Leitbilder-und-Handlungsstrategien-fuer-die-Raumentwicklung-in-Deutschland-2006.pdf, visited on 1. March 2007; 30 f

MKRO (= Geschäftsstelle der Ministerkonferenz für Raumordnung im Bundesministerium für Verkehr, Bau und Stadtentwicklung) (ed) (2006) Leitbilder und Handlungsstrategien für die Raumentwicklung in Deutschland [Visions and Strategies for Spatial Development in Germany]. Available online: http://www.bmvbs.de/Anlage/original_982048/Leitbilder-und-Handlungsstrategien-fuer-die-Raumentwicklung-in-Deutschland-2006.pdf, visited on 01.03.2007

OJ (= Official Journal of the European Union) 2006/L 210/19, Regulation (EC) No 1082/2006 of the European Parliament and the Council of 5 July 2006 on a European Grouping of territorial cooperation (EGTC). Available online: http://ec.europa.eu/regional_policy/sources/docoffic/official/regulation/pdf/2007/gect/ce_1082(2006)_en.pdf#search=%22%20european%20grouping%20territorial%20EGTC%22, visited on 23.08.2006

OJ (= Official Journal of the European Union) 2006/L 291/11, Council Decision of 6 October 2006 on Community strategic guidelines on cohesion (2006/702/EC). Available online: http://ec.europa.eu/regional_policy/sources/docoffic/2007/osc/l_29120061021en00110032 pdf, visited on 01.03.2007

Implementation of the EU Community Initiative INTERREG III A at the Polish-German border

An attempt at evaluation

Stanisław Ciok, Andrzej Raczyk

Departament of Spatial Management, Institute of Geography and Regional Development, Wrocław University, Wrocław

1 Introduction

Cross-border cooperation in the border area between Poland and Germany has the longest history on the national Polish scale and therefore is often treated as an example of a model solution, adapted to the realities of other border areas across the country. Poland's accession to the European Union and the introduction of the Community Initiative INTERREG III A into its border areas brought about significant changes, in scale as well as in forms of institutional cooperation.

The development of cross-border cooperation between Poland and Germany in the pre-accession period has been widely documented in the literature. However, descriptions concentrate mainly on its institutional character. Relatively few studies are dedicated to complex evaluation of the social, economic and spatial impacts of integration (Gorzelak et al. 2004, Ciok 2005). Thus, knowledge of the field is sparse and limited to the certain Euroregions or voivodships.

This study examines the impact of these changes on the scope and character of cooperation and undertakes a practical evaluation of the realization of cross-border cooperation programmes. The evaluation is based on a generic analysis of thematic priorities, the institutional structure of programme beneficiaries, and the compliance of particular projects with the principles of the European Union and national policies. The relationships between the spatial distribution of the programmes in progress and the level of social-economic development in particular areas are also examined.

2 Institutional aspects of Polish-German cross-border cooperation in the frame of INTERREG III A

Polish border areas, due to their peripheral location – and the consequences arising from it –, are usually regarded as underdeveloped and needful of activation (Ciok 2003a).

The relatively low level of economic development in border areas usually has various causes. Firstly, it may arise from the initial low level of development. Secondly, it may be the result of changes in the alignment of the border or its function. Because these types of areas are located on the periphery, and thus remote from economic and decision-making centres, they are less competitive and attractive for the influx of new investment and capital. They are often unable to overcome their backwardness. One possibility is to seek external aid. These are among the areas on which EU regional policy focuses (Churski 2002). With a view to developing border areas and supporting cross-border cooperation, the European Union has launched special programmes and allotted special funds (Ciok 2003b).

Depending on the location of border areas, special support programmes were created for them: the Community Initiative INTERREG III for EU Member States countries and – until EU enlargement in 2004 – the PHARE programme for Central-Eastern European candidate countries (European Commission 1998).

INTERREG III covered the years 2000-2006. Its function was to finance cross-border (strand A), transnational (strand B) and interregional cooperation (strand C) across internal as well as external borders of the European Union. INTERREG III allotted nearly € 5 billion. Among the three strands, the vast majority (67%) was allocated for strand A, that is to support cross-border cooperation between neighbouring border areas. Among the areas of action to be given particular support were (European Commission 1999):

- promotion of urban, rural and coastal areas,
- support of small and medium-size enterprises,
- creation of new jobs,
- environmental protection,
- improvement of transportation systems, and
- activities boosting economic and social development activities.

Within the framework of INTERREG III A for the years 2000–2006, 53 programmes supporting cross-border cooperation between EU countries were approved. The majority of funds were allotted to the border areas between Spain / Portugal (€ 807 m), Saxony / Czech Republic (€ 181 m), Greece / Bulgaria (€ 170 m), Spain / Morocco (€ 169 m), and Ireland / Northern Ireland (€ 130).

After accession to the EU, the ten new members received over € 424 m between 2004 and 2006 through INTERREG. Poland received more than 46% of these funds, followed by Hungary and the Czech Republic with about 14% each.

In Poland, 80% of the total INTERREG funds of € 196.1 m were allocated to strand A, 14% to strand B, and 6% to strand C. In absolute terms approximately € 149 m were dedicated to supporting cross-border cooperation (strand A).

Funds were distributed on the following pattern, according to the National Development Plan:

- Approximately € 73 m in total or approximately € 24 m annually for Poland's western border regions,
- approximately € 15 m in total or approximately € 5 m annually for Poland's southern border regions adjacent to the Czech Republic, and € 9 m or € 3 m respectively for the regions adjacent to Slovakia,
- approximately € 52 m in total or approximately € 17 m annually for Poland's eastern and northern-eastern borders.

Poland's accession to the EU brought about significant changes in the formation of institutional systems for cross-border cooperation. The development of cooperation in the border area between Poland and Germany was supported before 2004 on the Polish side by funding from the EU programme PHARE Cross-Border Cooperation (PHARE CBC), whereas INTERREG III A could only be applied on the German side. The institutional system of cooperation created in Poland in this period was mainly based on Euroregions managing small project funds and the Implementing Authority for the PHARE CBC Programme, which was in charge of the programme nationwide, in addition to managing 'large' projects worth more than € 2 m.

Despite the indisputable achievements of PHARE-CBC, it should be emphasized that its effectiveness as a tool of integration and coherence turned out to be relatively low. Compatibility with the INTERREG III A programmes on the German side was seriously limited. Such a situation was due mainly to the failure to harmonize activities and procedures in the two programmes. True cross-border projects at the advanced level of co-operation – i.e., joint preparation, implementation and financing – also proved impossible at the time because INTERREG III A funds could be spent only on EU territory. Hence such cross-border projects were hardly ever realized (Guz-Vetter 2004).

However, the experience gained in this period resulted the entities responsible for realizing the programme realization in individual local authorities, districts, and the region becoming more actively engaged in the long-lasting development of Euroregions and the initiation of new projects. Knowledge about realizing cross-border projects was disseminated and numerous contacts were established with German partners.

Upon Poland's accession to the EU, the country's border areas were included in seven cross-border cooperation programmes for the implementation of INTERREG III A, three of which were at the western border.

- Zachodniopomorskie - Mecklenburg-Vorpommern / Brandenburg,
- Lubuskie – Brandenburg, and
- Lower Silesia – Saxony (see fig. 1).

This was accompanied by changes in the institutional systems realizing the programmes at both the national and the regional levels. They were needed to ensure inclusion of regional authorities in border area planning to cope with differences in requirements between the INTERREG III A and PHARE-CBC programmes. One of the most important issues in this regard was the necessity of creating joint German-Polish organizational structures, i.e., the Joint Managing Authority, the Joint Paying Authority, the Joint Technical Secretariat, the Joint Steering Committee, and the Joint Monitoring Committee (see fig. 2). The problems with this venture proved to be not introducing these institutional requirements into the Polish administrative system, but actually distributing competencies.

For project selection and evaluation procedures, the harmonized rules adopted nationwide on the implementation system at the regional level prescribed:

- regional contact points at the marshal's[3] office to assist applicants with filling in the forms and compiling the necessary documents,
- evaluation by the departments of the marshal's office in charge of the regional policy implementation of the conformity of project proposals with regional strategy,
- formal legal evaluation by voivodship[4] offices , and finally
- Euroregion-managed special small projects funds.

---

[3] The marshal is the head of self-government of a voivodship.

[4] The voivod is the regional representative of the central government, comparable to a district governor.

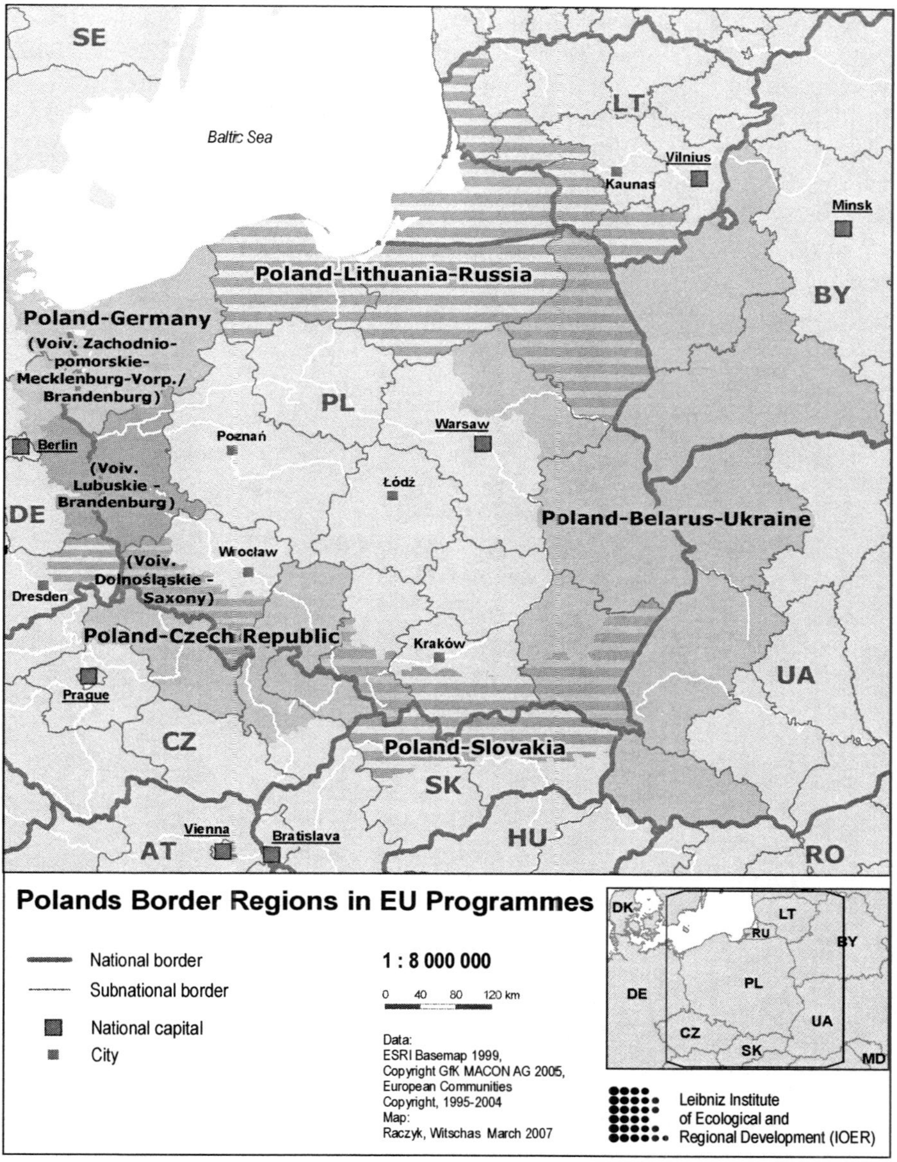

Figure 1. Spatial scope of the programmes carried out in Poland between 2004–2006 within the framework of Community Initiatives Interreg III A (Source: own study based on data from the Ministry of Regional Development)

The detailed distribution of competencies within a programme region was defined by individual agreements and varied across the country. The most important differences concerned the role of particular administrative units in project evaluation procedures. In the case of the Lower Silesia voivodship, a further organisation was included in the procedure, i.e., the Implementing Authority for the PHARE-CBC programme. The advantage of this arrangement was that it facilitated the professional approval applications by specialized authorities within the scope of their competencies. The main disadvantage, however, was complicate procedures and risk slowing down the whole verification process should one of the offices prove ineffective. The latter situation arose in the Lower Silesia voivodship, significantly delaying implementation of the programme.

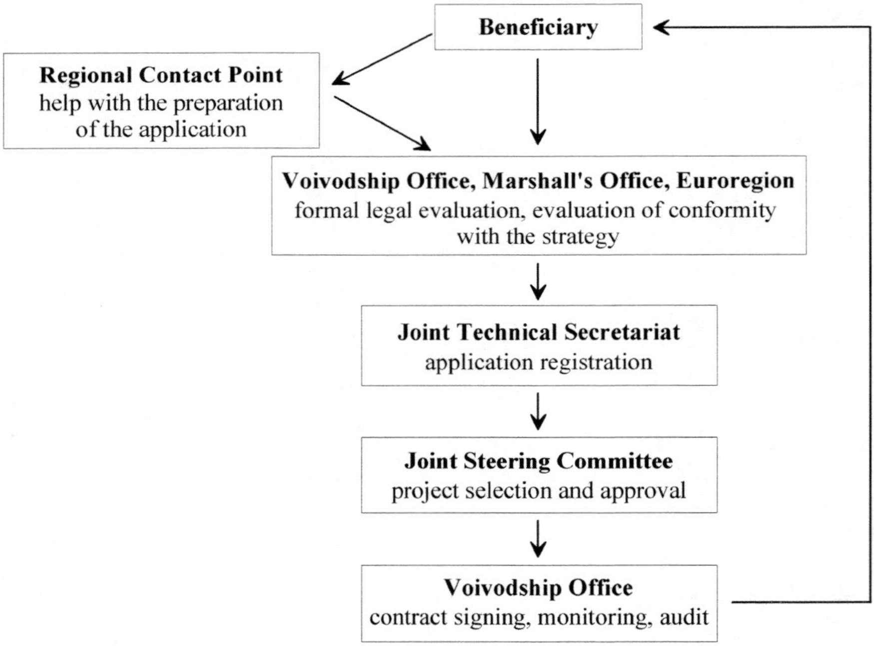

Figure 2. Project acquisition and evaluation procedure under Interreg III A programmes between 2004-2006 at the Polish-German border (Source: own study based on the data of the Ministry of Regional Development)

An important problem in creating joint implementation systems was that Poland joined the EU right in the middle of the 2000–2006 programming period. Including Poland in existing structures was simple in theory but in practice proved to be as difficult as creating such structures from scratch. This was because different legal systems in force on the two sides of the border had to be combined and to satisfy the requirements of the European

Commission. In the early stages, the problem was also exacerbated by insufficient knowledge among both Poles and Germans of the administrative system on the other side of the border. Different perceptions of the programme among all the organisations involved was a further source of difficulty.

Conversion from PHARE to INTERREG III A rules had far-reaching implications for the Euroregions. Beyond all doubt, the tremendous success of the idea of Euroregions, especially at Poland's western border, is rooted in their ability to tap EU funds, e.g., through the small projects fund. Affiliation with a Euroregion was a necessary precondition in applying for support under the small projects fund. In 2006, members of Euroregions no longer enjoyed preferential treatment in the process of project acquisition and evaluation because the geographical scope of INTERREG III A had shifted to NUTS 3 subregions. Therefore, a number of local authorities expressed doubts about the advisability of continued participation. The real threat of the Euroregion institutional crisis obliges them to seek other forms of activity, e.g., through participation in the programmes of other Structural Funds.

Another significant difference between PHARE and INTERREG III A programmes is the rule of cost reimbursement and a lack of an advance payment system as under INTERREG III A. Due to the length of funding reimbursement procedures, the beneficiaries must raise practically all the amounts needed to carry out a project. Such a situation selectively reduces potential applicants to entities in the best financial condition, which from a spatial point of view may further polarize levels of social-economic development in border areas.

One of the most important factors, mostly disregarded in all publications but crucial to the efficiency of programme administration, is its specificity, as well as its relative inexpensive as a regional policy tool. It is underestimated at both the central and national levels. In practice, it means that the INTERREG III A is treated as a less important funding scheme with the majority of effort and funding being devoted to implementing mainstream EU regional policy programmes. At the regional level, the result is an intensive drain of the staff involved in the programmes, especially in favour of the mainstream programmes. The lack of stable personnel and the resulting insufficient preparation lie at the heart of low administrative efficiency at the regional level.

Another important problem is the neglect or superficial treatment of cross-border cooperation in the most important planning documentation prepared for the central authorities such as the National Development Plan, the Integrated Regional Operational Programme, the Sectoral Operational

Programs or the the National Conception of Spatial Development (Kołodziejski & Szmigiel 2004).

3 Project evaluation

In order to evaluate cross-border cooperation apart from the specificity of the institutional system, account needs to be taken of the practical implications of realization. Since in most cases these programmes are still in the implementation phase and because it is barely possible to obtain information on the factual effects of particular initiatives, the projects approved for realization by the joint steering committees were analyzed. The analysis is thus based on the documentation of project applications. They do not include projects under 'technical assistance' priorities used for programme management and evaluation.

According to the approved programmes, the total amount of allocations for Polish cross-border areas in the years 2004-2006 within INTERREG III A was over € 86.6 m (€ 82.3 m without technical assistance). Due to considerable delays in the approval and realization of the three programmes, commencement of project acquisition was not announced till December 2004 and in the case of the Lower Silesia voivodship not until June 2005. The first steering committee decisions of the on the realization of individual projects were taken in March 2006. The next 130 projects were approved by the end of January 2006 and amounted to nearly € 44 m, which constituted 53% of total funding allocated to the programme. It reflected a significant interest among beneficiaries and effective administration structures, except for the Lower Silesia voivodship where, as we have seen, problems arose with the functioning of the institutional system.

It therefore seems that the limited capability of Polish regions to absorb the funds due to lack of sufficient own funds and poor knowledge of procedures among potential beneficiaries redicted by a number of authors (e.g Szlachta 2002; Grosse 2004) indicating were groundless. The rapid realization of projects was made possible mainly thanks to the considerable reduction in application preparation and processing time. While on the German side the average period for completion of a project – from idea to final approval by the steering committee – was between 6 and 9 months, on the Polish side it could be estimated at about 3–4 months. This was due partly to differences in the functioning of the implementation system on the two sides of the border. In Germany the beneficiary received support with project preparation virtually from the moment the general idea was born. By contrast, Polish beneficiaries had to have a more specific idea of the project from the beginning, since the help offered was mostly in correctly filling in forms and providing the necessary documentation.

These differences raised the probability of 'losing' valuable projects in the early stages of documentation preparation but at the same time meant fewer duties for overstretched administrative staff. The system used on the Polish side worked well when there was a great demand for projects, although in the event of eminent problems with the acquisition of future projects in relation to particular, specific priorities such as economic cooperation between enterprises, evolution towards the German system seems necessary.

Another reason why the time for preparing the applications was shorter in Poland than in Germany is that many Polish projects had already been submitted to the Integrated Regional Operational Programme in the frame of the European Regional Development Fund (ERDF), but had been rejected. Some of these projects were simply modified to suit the transborder effect requirements and re-submitted unter INTERREG III A. However, especially in the early period, this led to poor quality in the cross-border cooperation of projects.

Among the initiatives realized, the majority required a relatively low subsidy of less than € 250.000. The projects, according to the value of investment, were highly diverse. The biggest financial outlays were for infrastructure projects, the smallest ones for 'soft' projects concerning cultural cooperation and the development of human resources.

Due to the diversity of priorities and the functioning of the particular programmes at the western border, generic analysis of the projects was based on the intervention categories used by the European Commission in the monitoring and reporting process. The majority of the projects were carried out in the areas of tourism, transportation infrastructure, social, environmental as well as telecommunications infrastructure, and in the development of rural areas – together constituting over 70% of the total.

The clear dominance of infrastructure-related projects suggests that despite the long experience gathered in a number of previous programmes, cross-border cooperation is still in its infancy and, this being they case, concerned with creating material bases for cooperating. However, this would be a gross simplification, since project structure on the Polish side is largely determined by the great need for investment. This is due to the long-term negligence of border areas and the consequent very low level of development, especially in comparison with the German side. It should not be forgotten that the Poland-German border is one of the internal borders of the European Union that displays the greatest difference in levels of economic development between neighbouring countries (ESPON Secretariat 2004).

The scale of diversity very often causes divergent aims and expectations, which obviously create problems in implementing joint Polish-German projects. This is also because local and regional authorities on the Polish side of the border attach too much significance to infrastructure investment. Although material bases for cooperation have to be created and differences in levels of economic development eliminated on the two sides of the border, the scope of intervention must be gradually extended. Above all, the Implementation Authority should put more stress on promoting initiatives in the field of human resources, cooperation between economic entities – including SME sector, technological research and development, spatial planning, and the reconstruction of degraded regions. This would improve the quality of cooperation between neighbouring countries in border areas.

Taking into account the spatial distribution of particular projects, 60% of projects were carried out in urban areas, i.e., measures were implemented there. About 10% of initiatives encompassed both urban and rural areas. This asymmetry was evident in practically all intervention categories and was due to urban areas being the main links in cooperation. What is noticeable is the dominance of the biggest towns in the border area such as Szczecin, Zielona Góra and Gorzów Wielkopolski and their immediate neighbours in the distribution of the projects. Proximity to the border was a secondary factor in these cases. Such spatial distribution may indicate the formalized nature of cooperation, initiated mostly by marshal's offices, the decision centres – or point to dependency on information. It may also be the result of institutions in these areas being best prepared to submit appropriate applications quickly. The apparent interdependency between the size of particular entities, their administrative status and the size of projects realized may indicate the existence of a barrier in access to funds.

In order to investigate the main factors determining the spatial distribution of the entities involved, the authors compared the arithmetic mean of values for the population of the local authorities implementing projects and those that did not in relation to certain social-economic indicators. Levene's test for equality of variances was the method applied (Nawojczyk 2002).

The research showed that the most conspicuous differences between the two populations were in factors defining the level of economic development (the entrepreneurial factor, the level of development of the service sector, the affluence of the companies and the inhabitants). An important role in determining the possibilities of participation in the programme was played by the financial independence of local authorities, which to a great extent the outcome of economic developments such as local government income and share per capita in national tax revenues. Taking into consideration autonomous local authorities' dominance in the group of programme beneficiaries, the local authority quality was of great significance. The indicator used here was councillors' level of education.

Thus, the richest municipalities with significant financial resources and a good economic situation, as well as a favourable labour market structure had the greatest chances of obtaining EU funds. Impoverished entities burdened with significant expenditure on social aid benefited much less frequently from the programme. What is more, such dependencies, although not so apparent, were also confirmed within subpopulations of urban municipalities, urban-rural municipalities and rural authorities. This situation will obviously augment intraregional diversification in the future.

Evaluating the quality of particular projects is the most important but most difficult task in analysing the effectiveness of particular programmes. In relation to EU policies, the vast majority of projects was qualified as neutral with respect to the environment (over 70%), gender equality (over 80%), and creation of the information society (nearly 90%). Their added value in this aspect was therefore relatively low.

The real transborder effect of projects needs also to be critically assessed. In nearly one third of cases it was limited to the joint preparation of the project, which in practice meant gaining support from the German partner. In over half the projects, a German partner participated in both the preparation and the realization stages. It should be stressed, however, that this participation was in many cases only declared, or took the form of formalized contacts between institutions, meaning there was very little real cooperation. Only 7% of the projects could be classified as advanced cooperation. They took the form of 'mirror' projects, realized on both sides of the border and addressing the same issues. Due to formal legal determinants, Polish-German programmes did not involve projects with a lead partner, in which the beneficiary managed projects covering the areas on the other side of the border.

The low transborder effect of the projects examined resulted, above all, from their generic structure, i.e., the dominance of infrastructure investment, in which a partner on the other side of the border was not even required. It was also partly the result of the specific structure of programme beneficiaries, with a clear dominance of local and regional authorities, over three-quarters of the all beneficiaries. They had significant difficulty realizing projects of a clearly transborder nature because of formal legal requirements such as the lack of possibilities for co-financing projects implemented on the German side of the border, annual budget planning, etc.

Other important issues were low awareness of the significance of the transborder effect in the activities realized within INTERREG III A, as well as the difficulty local and regional authorities in defining the very notion of transborder effects. Most frequently they were associated with having a partner on the other side of the border, which was the result of implementation practice at the time of the PHARE CBC programmes. Consequently, the projects realized had relatively little impact on real cross-border cooperation, which undermines the main idea of the INTERREG III programme.

The important problems in implementing the INTERREG III A programme arise from the common perception of the area on the other side of the border among the inhabitants and the regional authorities in terms of competition rather than cooperation (Leśniak 2006). It is largely due to historical conditions and functional similarity of these areas. This has hindered the development of links and economic integration. Retaining the current structure of beneficiaries may also cause excessive institutionalization and formalization of the programme. It is therefore advisable to undertake a wide range of activities to include SME sector and other non-governmental organizations in cooperation programmes. It requires a lot of activities to promote the programmes and civic society. Changing the structure of beneficiaries may help reduce potential for excessive disparities arising in the spatial and social-economic development of the border areas.

4 Conclusions

Analysis of the implementation of the INTERREG III A programmes at Poland's western borders allows the following conclusions:

- Selection and evaluation procedures are overly complicated, owing mainly to legal regulations. Procedures need to be simplified and based on a clear division of competencies.
- In the future, Euroregions may play an important role in the process of border-area integration, while marshals' offices will continue to play the dominant role, and the quality and pace of integration will depend on them.
- The lack of stable administrative structures and high turnover in the staff involved in the programme at both the regional and central levels constitute a significant problem. It is hard to determine with certainty

whether this is a temporary situation arising from the conscious development of programme structures from scratch, or a consequence of the instability typical of such institutions.

- One of the most important mental challenges facing border area inhabitants is to raise their awareness of living in a border area. Partners on the other side of the border also need to be involved more strongly as the synergy effect arising from cooperation exceeds the benefits of competition.
- The realization of cooperation programmes may cause further polarization within the border area.
- It would be advisable to change the structure of projects by reducing the number of infrastructural projects in favour of projects oriented on the formation of social capital and social and economic integration.
- The activation of cooperation between business entities and the organizations of the non-profit sector seems necessary.
- The projects realized must be the effect of conscious activities by the regional authorities responsible for regional policy. This requires the development of advanced planning and study concepts for the border area by the scientific community.
- Further research needs to be conducted into the identification of the transborder effect beyond the simple product, result or impact factors used in descriptions of the projects.

The funds allocated to cross-border cooperation within the New Financial Perspective 2007–2013 in accordance with the suggestions of the Ministry of Regional Development will probably remain at the current level. Therefore, projects will have to pay greater attention to cross-border effects and significantly contribute to their development. This is the direction in which the legal changes proposed by the European Commission point: projects are to be realized in mutual cooperation between beneficiaries from two different countries on at least four planes: joint preparation, joint implementation, joint staff, joint financing (European Parliament 2006). Approval of these proposals will significantly increase the formal requirements and difficulties in the use of accessible funds. The current model of cooperation in the Polish-German border area will also have to be modified.

References

Churski P (2002) Problem areas and support areas in polish regional policy. In: Ciok S, Ilnicki D (eds) The Transformation of Regional Spatial-Functional

Structures. Regional aspect of European integration. University of Wroclaw, Institute of Geography and Regional Development, Wroclaw

Ciok S (2003a) Wykorzystanie środków programu PHARE-CBC dla rozwoju pogranicza polsko-niemieckiego [Absorption of PHARE-CBC funds for development of polish-german cross-border area]. In: Klasik A (ed) Zarządzanie rozwojem lokalnym i regionalnym w kontekście integracji europejskiej [Local and regional management in the context of european integration]. Polish Academy of Sciences, Warsaw, 155–170

Ciok S (2003b) The Financing of international cross-border cooperation between Central- and East- European Countries by the European Union. Geopolitical Studies 11, 405–413

Ciok S (2004) Pogranicze polsko-niemieckie. Problemy współpracy transgranicznej [Cross-border area. Problems of cross-border cooperation]. Acta Universitatis Wratislaviensis No 2603. University of Wroclaw, Wroclaw

European Commission (1998): Commission Regulation (EC) No 2760/98 of 18 December 1998 concerning the implementation of a programme for cross-border cooperation in the framework of the PHARE programme, Brussels, 1998

European Commission (1999): Council Regulation (EC) No 1260/1999 of 21 June 1999 laying down general provisions on the Structural Funds, Brussels, 1999

European Parliament (2006): Regulation (EC) no 1080/2006 of the European Parliament and of the Council of 5 July 2006 on the European Regional Development Fund and repealing Regulation (EC) No 1783/1999, Brussels, 2006

ESPON Secretariat (2004) Espon in progress – Preliminary results by autumn 2003. European Spatial Planning Observation Network, Luxembourg

Gorzelak G, Bachtler J, Kasprzyk M (2004) Współpraca transgraniczna Unii Europejskiej: Doświadczenia Polski i Niemiec [Cross-border Co-operation of the European Union: Experiences of Germany and Poland]. Wyd. Naukowe "Scholar", Warsaw

Grosse T M (2004) Opportunities and threats of absorption of UE funds. Regional and Local Studies 1(15)/2004, Warsaw

Guz-Vetter M (2004) Współpraca transgraniczna Polska – Niemcy finansowana z programów PHARE Cross Border Co-operation i Interreg III A. Dotychczasowe doświadczenia i nowe wyzwania [Polish - German cross – border cooperation financed by Phare and INTERREG IIIA. Experiences and new challenges]. In: Ciok S, Ilnicki D (eds) Przekształcenia regionalnych struktur funkcjonalno – przestrzennych. Regionalny wymiar integracji europejskiej [The Transformation of Regional Spatial-Functional Structures. Regional aspect of European integration]. University of Wroclaw, Institute of Geography and Regional Development, Wroclaw, 377–386

Kołodziejski M, Szmigiel K (2004) Międzynarodowa współpraca transgraniczna i międzyregionalna w kontekście polityki regionalnej państwa na lata 2007–2013. Ekspertyza na zlecenie Departamentu Polityki Regionalnej [Transnational, interregional and cross-border cooperation in context of regional policy for 2007–2013. Analyse for Regional Policy Department]. Local Development Centre, Warsaw

Leśniak N (2005) Konkurencyjność pogranicza polsko-niemieckiego [Competitiveness of Polish-German cross-border area]. University of Wroclaw, Institute of Geography and Regional Development, Wroclaw

Nawojczyk M (2002) Przewodnik po statystyce dla socjologów [Guide sociologist through statistics]. SPSS Poland, Krakow

Szlachta J (2002) Znaczenie funduszy europejskich dla rozwoju regionalnego Polski [Role of European Funds for Polish regional development. Poland and EU], Regional Centre of European Integration, Torun

II Cross-border governance at regional level

Cross-border co-operation in the Rhine-Scheldt Delta
The long road of institution building

Jochem de Vries

Department of Human Geography, Planning and International Development Studies; Faculty of Social and Behavioural Sciences, University of Amsterdam

1 Introduction

In 1927 the Dutch parliament failed to ratify a treaty with Belgium on the Moerdijk canal. This canal would have given the Belgian port of Antwerp a good connection with the river Rhine on Dutch territory. The Dutch senate did not ratify the treaty because Belgian claims to Dutch territory had caused a lot of unrest in the Netherlands. This was precisely the reason why the Dutch government negotiated the deal in the first place. It wanted to ease tension in relations with the southern neighbour. This was needed because an influential Belgian movement in the inter bellum period advocated annexation of large parts of the southern Netherlands by Belgium (Ruys 1996). Antwerp had to wait until 1975 before a canal that connected the port with the Rhine was opened.

Already before World War II, relations between the Netherlands and Belgium improved, but the war really brought the countries together, almost literally because both governments were in exile in London. The ties created in London developed into the Benelux Economic Union (BEU), which was established by treaty in 1958. The economic integration of both countries (and Luxembourg) was already nearly completed in 1970 and was far in advance of the European Union (then European Community). Benelux internal border controls were already abolished in the nineteen sixties. There are few neighbouring countries with such good relations, historical ties, and a common language to compare with Belgium and the Netherlands. It is remarkable that the sporadic diplomatic tensions between the two countries often concern issues in the physical environment.

In the nineteenth and twentieth centuries, modernisation and the formation of nation-states led to hard borders. These borders have become important structuring devices for diverse social practices. The changing relations between Belgium and The Netherlands summarized above imply that borders gradually lose their toughness (De Vries 2002a). This means that the Dutch-Belgium border region approaches what Martinez (1994) describes as *integrated borderlands*. In his classification – of four classes – this is the type of border area in which cross-border relationships are the most intense and the least antagonistic. “Stability is strong and permanent. Economies of both countries are functionally merged and there is unrestricted movement of people and goods across the boundary. Borderlands perceive themselves as members of one social system” (Martinez 1994: 3)

While in theory the Dutch-Flemish border area is mounting in the hierarchy proposed by Martinez, in practice integration on a cross-border regional scale is not so straightforward. For some activities – such as shopping – people frequently do cross borders. For other activities – such as education and health facilities – this is far more limited (Knippenberg 2004). This shows that the relationship between the two countries has improved dramatically in half a century on the macro-level of the state. Major, fundamental tensions on territorial questions have been replaced by far-reaching cooperation and integration. Nevertheless, cross-border integration on a regional scale is clearly lagging.

Already in the nineteen sixties, there were first moves to establish cross-border cooperation in spatial planning. In the nineteen nineties there was a sharp increase in initiatives as a result of European integration. Nevertheless, cross-border cooperation has not yet become a success story (De Vries 2000b).

This contribution discusses the extent of governmental integration across borders in the Dutch-Belgian border region. It focuses on governance structures and policies concerning the physical environment. The theoretical perspective chosen is institutional capacity building. The literature on institutional capacity building (see e.g. Healey 1997) emphasises the importance of the institutional context for concrete decision-making. Institutions are to be understood as a broad category of characteristics that facilitate the interaction between actors. These can be soft cultural traits such as a common (policy) language or hard traits such as a legal framework. The general idea is that the more institutions are shared by a group of actors the easier their interaction will be. Furthermore, besides solving a concrete issue – such as cross-border negotiations on road or rail links – interaction between actors can contribute to the creation of institutions.

In general, the institutional context has three dimensions: A social, knowledge, and political dimension. The social dimension consists of the amount and nature of durable relationships between actors. Intensive relationships and trust are favourable pre-conditions for solving issues between stakeholders. Shared knowledge in an actor network is the second dimension of institutional capacity. Important is not only the existence and availability of knowledge also its acceptance by members of the network. The third dimension of the institutional context is the capacity to act. This political dimension refers to the tools available in the network to implement policy objectives. (Healey 1997)

This contribution examines how different initiatives in the Rhine-Scheldt Delta contribute to the cross-border institutional capacity to solve physical environment issues.

The dominance of national borders has lead to a situation in which cross-border institutional capacity is very limited. The next section sketches the spatial characteristics of the Rhine-Scheldt Delta. The subsequent section describes the spectrum of cooperation. The contribution concludes with a brief analysis from the institutional capacity building perspective.

2 The Rhine-Scheldt Delta explored[5]

The geographical focus of this contribution is an area referred to as the Rhine-Scheldt Delta. It is bordered by the North Sea coast and a semicircle formed by the cities of Rotterdam, Dordrecht, Breda, Antwerp, Ghent and Bruges. The border between the Netherlands and Belgium runs east-west through the area (see fig. 1) (Benelux 1997). Three large European river basins, the Scheldt, the Meuse and the Rhine, discharge into the North Sea in this region. This has resulted in a peninsular structure with large gradients from fresh to salt water. From an ecological point of view, the estuaries are very valuable. From the point of view of safety, the delta, of which considerable parts are below sea level, is vulnerable to flooding. The 1953 flood in which 1800 people lost their lives is still an important frame of reference. The structure with the large rivers is also the reason why the re-

[5] This section is based on De Vries et al. (2001) and Romein et al. (2001).

gion once was dubbed the Golden Delta. Waterway-related economic activities contribute greatly to the region's wealth (De Vries et al. 2001).

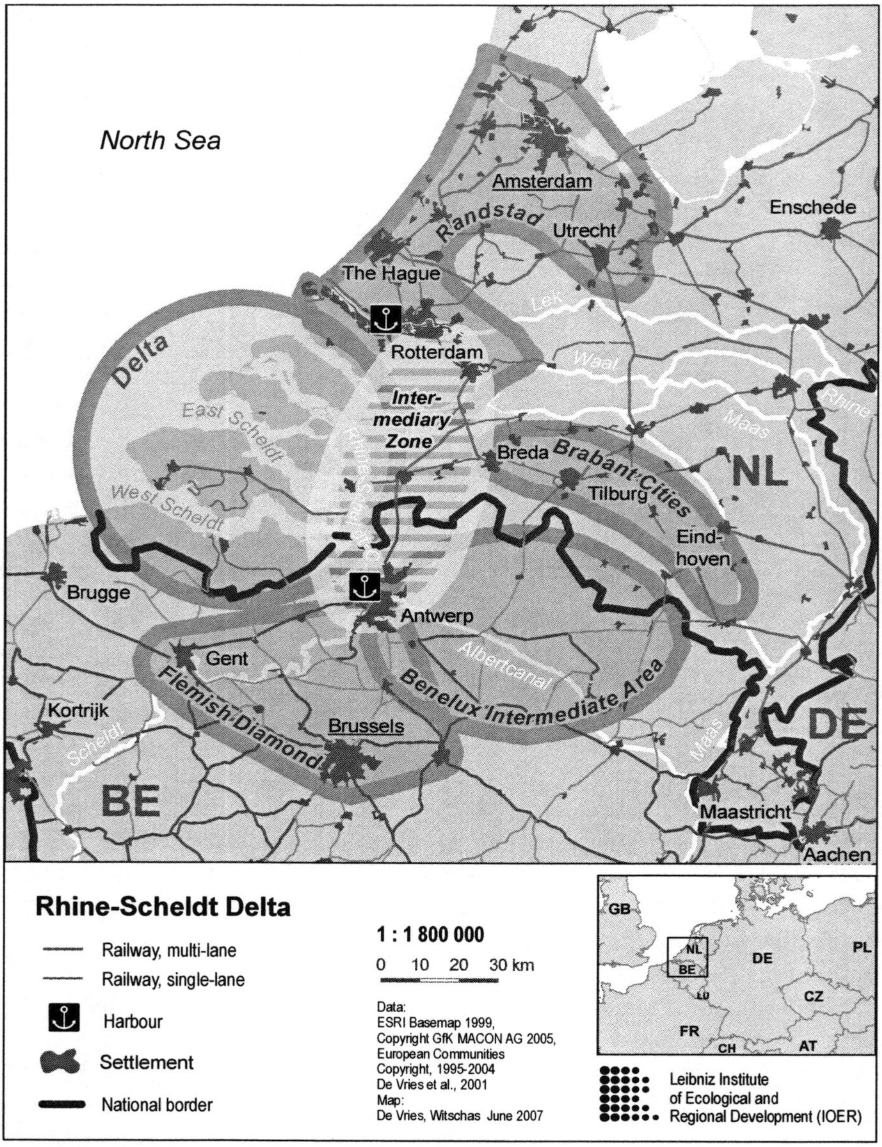

Figure 1. The Rhine-Scheldt Delta

The second characteristic of the delta of relevance for cross-border co-operation is the occupancy pattern. The region can be roughly subdivided into a number of areas (De Vries et al. 2001: 58). The region is bordered to the south by the core polycentric urban region of Flanders – the Flemish Diamond and to the north by that of the Netherlands – Randstad[6]. To the north of the Flemish Diamond and to the south of the Randstad, land-use functions and patterns are heavily influenced by the two port complexes, which both rank among the largest in the world. The area between Rotterdam (south of Dordrecht) and Antwerp forms an intermediary zone, which is much more difficult to classify than the areas surrounding it. Although many places in this zone have above average urbanization rates, it is still relatively open. On the Dutch side, overspill from the Rotterdam Mainport area can be observed. Large-scale activities in particular, sometimes polluting, have found their way into this area, where the struggle for land is less fierce than around Rotterdam, and access to infrastructure is excellent. This development, described by locals as 'beautiful West Brabant turning into a conveyor belt of tarmac, steel and concrete' causes a lot of dissatisfaction (Romein et al, 2001). On the Flemish side, the intermediary zone is also relatively open, despite an urbanization rate above the average for Flanders. The area north of Antwerp is well wooded but heavily fragmented by residential development. A proportion of the demand for housing is of Dutch origin. In addition to the fiscal attraction of the area for some Dutch households, the size of houses and plots lures them across the border.

To the west of the intermediary zone, the archipelago of peninsulas is still very rural in nature and its few cities are relatively small. There is some harbour activity on the West Scheldt, but everywhere else the water and adjacent land is predominantly the domain of tourism and nature. Obviously, beach tourism and yachting are important and attract national and international tourists.

Third, the main characteristic of the regions infrastructure is a relatively narrow North-South bundle of internationally connecting infrastructure (the Intermediary Zone). This includes a waterway – The Rhine-Scheldt Canal –, a system of motorways, traditional rail lines and, in the near future, a high speed rail link between Rotterdam and Antwerp (2007). This corridor of north-south infrastructure – in the intermediate area – is wedged between two areas where north-south infrastructure is at a considerably lower level. It is unlikely that the infrastructure in neighbouring

[6] The Flemish Diamond is the name Flemish planners developed for the urban region of which Louvain, Brussels, Gand and Antwerp are main cities. In the Netherlands Randstad or 'Rim City' is a familiar name to refer to the cities in the Western Netherlands of which Rotterdam, The Hague, Amsterdam and Utrecht are the most important (Albrechts 2001).

areas will be upgraded in the near future. In the case of the peninsulas, ecological considerations will prevent upgrading, while the Benelux intermediate area is an unlikely place to accommodate north-south flows. As a result, it is most likely that the zone between Antwerp and Rotterdam will have to accommodate the increased flow. Whether existing infrastructure will be expanded and new infrastructure built in the most sustainable way depends very much on cross-border coordination.

Fourth, east-west infrastructure is found to the south and north of the Rhine-Scheldt Delta. Both to the north south of the region, these east-west zones of infrastructure include all modes of transport and provide important international connections. This structure is very much the result the ports of Rotterdam and Antwerp having developed and continuing to develop their hinterland infrastructure separately. Despite European policies such as the Trans European Networks, the national perspective on infrastructure development is still prevalent. As a result infrastructure is invested in on both sides of the border with no serious consideration being given to the alternative of realizing infrastructure together. A recent example is the simultaneous completion on both sides of the border of a dedicated freight rail line connecting the ports of Antwerp and Rotterdam to the German hinterland. On the Dutch side, the newly built Betuwe railway has been much debated with regard to cost-effectiveness and environmental impact. On the Flemish side, the upgrading of an unused railway has been planned which, as the Belgian answer to Rotterdam's natural hinterland connection, is fittingly called the Iron Rhine. This much cheaper alternative has not been completed because the Dutch government has thus far declined to become involved in the project, having a say because a small stretch of the line crosses into Dutch territory.

The fifth important characteristic of the Rhine-Scheldt Delta is the Scheldt River as a waterway. This river forms the sea entrance for the port of Antwerp. A larger part of the river and the estuary between the sea and the port is Dutch territory. The right of unrestricted entrance to the port for shipping was guaranteed by the treaty in 1839 that settled the division of the Netherlands and Belgium. Nevertheless, issues regarding the management of the Scheldt between Antwerp and the sea are severely complicated by the existence of the state border.

Last but not least, the relatively open area around the border, which is a typical borderland phenomenon, should be mentioned. Woodlands are to be found on the sandy soil to the east. On the Dutch side, they are predominantly located close to the border region. In fact these woodlands form a larger area that is relatively sparsely populated, stretching further to the east. As a result of being a peripheral area from a national perspective, less development pressure exists in border areas than in many other places in the same country. Of course all this can change when internal borders within the EU further lose their importance (which today is not completely the case as has been suggested in the first section).

It can be concluded that a wide variety of issues stemming from the spatial characteristics of the Rhine Scheldt Delta give rise to cross-border tensions. Territorial competition between the main ports leads to an uneconomical use of land and infrastructure. Conflicts between economic and ecological interests have an important cross-border dimension. The realization of cross-border infrastructure plays an important role in the region.

3 Patchwork of governance structures[7]

Over time, a broad range of different initiatives for cooperation have emerged in the Rhine-Scheldt Delta region. They show quite a wide variety in geographical scope, functional orientation, number and type of actors, the extent of formalisation, and modes of operation. Without claiming to give an exhaustive overview, this section should provide a good idea of the variety of initiatives (see table 1).

3.1 Border commission VlaNed

The Border commission Flanders-South Netherlands (acronym VlaNed) is part of the Benelux Economic Union. This commission covers a large part of the Dutch-Belgian border. It is strictly a network of civil servants of the Dutch national government and the Flemish regional and provincial governments on both sides of the border. The commission focuses on spatial planning – *ruimtelijke ordening* – as defined in the Netherlands and Flanders.

In 1969, spatial planning was added to the mission of Benelux. As a result, a commission was installed to coordinate spatial structure plans on both sides of the border. This task was reinforced by an official decision of the Benelux ministers in 1974, which made mutual cross-border consultation about structure plans compulsory[8]. In 2003 it was decided to revitalise this agreement by developing a protocol for consultation. One precondition under this protocol is the appointment of a contact person within each organisation.

---

7 This section has benefited from BEU (2005).

8 The BEU can take binding decisions in order to implement the Benelux treaty.

Table 1. Overview of cross-border cooperation in the area of spatial development

	Border commission VlaNed	Euregions	ProSes	RSD-cooperation	Others
EU involvement	No involvement	Strong: determines framework conditions	Restricted: mainly through Birds and Habitat directives	Very limited	Very limited
BEU involvement	Leading	No involvement	Moderate: facilitating consensus building as a mediator	Strong in establishing the initiative; limited in running the cooperation	Involved in many initiatives and performing different roles
Scope	Broad: spatial development at large	Broad: regional development, divers issues, fragmented	Restricted, clearly defined: sea accessibility of the Antwerp harbour, nature development and protection from flooding	Broad: regional development at large	Wide variety in area of regional development; varying from policy coordination, maintenance, and project development
Policy instruments	Communicative: backed by BEU guideline on mutual consultation on statutory spatial plans	Financial: EU subsidies matched by grants from local and regional governments	Legal: agreements are fixed through international treaties. Financial: Dutch national government and Flemish regional government investments	Communicative: setting agendas for cross-border projects and starting these regional cooperation projects	Most of the time informal agreements. Regional and local financial contribution on a case by case basis
Status	Permanent	Semi-permanent, based on INTERREG programmes	Project based	Semi-Permanent: network organisation	—
Interconnections**	Many	Limited	Moderate	Many	—

* This table does not pretend to provide a complete overview.

** The extent to which coordination exists with other forms of cross-border cooperation.

Until recently, the commission was the exclusive domain of governments, but recently representatives of other cross-border co-operation schemes, such as Euregions and the Rhine-Scheldt Delta cooperation, have been granted observer status. When the commission was installed in 1969, it was explicitly mentioned that governments would be represented at the level of directors. In practice, lower ranking civil servants step in. The commission meets twice a year. The emphasis in discussions is on plans with legal status, which in practice means the exchange of information about plans in the spatial planning system and hence not plans from adjacent sectors. Over the last few years, the commission has broadened its scope by developing its own programme and not only letting the flow of official plans dictate the agenda of meetings. In developing the programme, the commission has more actively involved politically responsible actors. While direct influence of the commission on policies let alone spatial development should not be exaggerated, its contribution is mostly in the social dimension of institutional capacity building. The fact that the commission has a relatively long tradition and meets on a regular basis is an important contribution to the establishment and maintenance of a cross-border network of planning officials. The Secretariat-General of BEU – the BEU officials – acts as secretary of this commission. Its role in sustaining the work of this commission cannot be underestimated.

3.2 Euregions

In the border region Rhine Scheldt-Delta, there are two Euregions: Scheldemond and Benelux Middengebied. The Euregions are an important lynchpin between the European Union and regional governments in border regions. They function as organs that implement EU policies, while the EU does not have decentralised agencies of its own (Perkmann 1998). On the request of the European Commission, which is interested in establishing large-scale European regions, the Euregions Benelux Middengebied and Scheldemond have submitted a joint programme for the INTERREG III A programme (2002 - 2008) the border region Flanders -The Netherlands. The Euregions Scheldemond and Benelux Middengebied are both based legally on the Benelux Agreement on Cross-border Cooperation[9] (1986), which offers different types of legal construction for cross-border co-operation. On the basis of this agreement between the Benelux countries, a

9 Benelux Overeenkomst inzake Grensoverschrijdende Samenwerking tussen Territoriale Samenwerkingsverbanden of Autoriteiten / Convention Benelux Concernant la Coopération Transfrontalière entre Collectivités ou Autorités Territoriales – Signed in Brussels September 12, 1986

cross-border cooperation initiative can obtain the status of an independent corporate body, which in general increases its room for discretion.

Both Euregions are strongly focussed on (cross-border) regional economic development. The main mode of operation is for projects implemented by third parties to be subsidised. A joint programme sets out the criteria for projects. Third parties can be governments as well as private parties.

Projects are generally on a small scale and only partly geared towards the physical environment. Projects concerned with the physical environment are small-scale infrastructure projects, regional economic ventures, cultural and historical activities, and water management. Besides the limited funds available, the time horizon of the programme – as dictated by the EU – allows little scope for larger and hence longer term projects.

From an institutional capacity building point of view, the political dimension can be said to be relatively well developed. The budget for both Euregions together amounts to € 82 million from the European Commission for the period 2002-2008. In agreement with the European mode of operation this amount has to be matched by the same amount from the region itself. To put this in perspective: the Rhine-Scheldt Delta Cooperation has a budget of € 500.000 for the year 2005.

3.3 Project Team Development Perspective Scheldt Estuary (ProSes)

Compared with other initiatives along the Flemish-Dutch border, cooperation around the Scheldt estuary is relatively far-reaching. The Scheldt is the entrance to the harbour of Antwerp, an ecological valuable area and a notorious apple of discord between the Netherlands and Flanders. With the signing of a treaty between the Netherlands and Flanders[10] about the widening and dredging of a shipping channel, a long stalemate has given way to constructive cooperation. This deadlock could only be broken after the issue of the Scheldt was linked with another dossier: the high speed train link (HSL) from Rotterdam to Antwerp. While this has never been officially confirmed, the Netherlands undertook to cooperate with Flanders on the Scheldt dossier while in the case of the HSL it would be the other way around. Part of the agreement on widening the waterway was that an envi-

[10] Within the federal state of Belgium, the Flemish region is a quasi-sovereign authority with respect to issues concerning the physical environment such as spatial planning and water management.

ronmental compensation programme. Elaboration of these agreements has gradually led to a more far-reaching cooperation.

In 2001, after preparatory work by a Dutch-Flemish working party, a project directorate was installed. This project organisation of around forty people has prepared a development perspective for the Scheldt-estuary (ProSes), a vision of the desired development of the Scheldt estuary including an implementation programme closing linking between access to the port of Antwerp, flood control, and rehabilitation of the ecosystem.

With the signing of a memorandum of agreement, the Dutch and Flemish governments have committed themselves to a range of measures until 2010. They include strengthening dikes and levees, the establishing floodplains, widening the waterway, and nature projects. The total estimated costs are € 1.3 billion . It should be noted that much investment is not directly dependent on cross-border agreement, but could and would have been realised by Flanders in any case. Nevertheless, for preparation alone – prior to any work being implemented – the Dutch-Flemish project organisation has € 60 million to its disposal.

As far as the geographical scale of the project is concerned, it is clearly a border regional project. Cooperation is essentially between two central governments – in the Netherlands the national government and in Flanders the regional government. The latter being quasi-sovereign in matters of spatial planning and water management, it cooperates on an equal footing with the Dutch national government. Furthermore, meso-governments – provinces – have an advisory role.

The Benelux secretary-general acted as secretary of this advisory council. By definition, the project organisation has a limited life span, but careful steps are being taken to make cooperation durable. One such idea is to create a Scheldt landscape park[11].

3.4 Rhine-Scheldt Delta Cooperation

While ProSes is largely a top-down initiative, Rhine-Scheldt cooperation is, by contrast a *bottom-up* initiative. It officially started in 1995 with the signing of the declaration of intent by Dutch and Flemish parties. Over the years, a network organisation developed with around 40 parties. These parties include provinces, municipalities, the Dutch national government, the Flemish regional government, chambers of commerce, port authorities, environmental organisations, and the BEU. The network organisation has a

[11] Based on the example of the Emscher landscape park (D'hondt a. Van Huut 2005), a project that transformed the industrial sites of the Ruhr District.

small secretariat which is headed by a 'Delta manager'. Officially, cooperation is informal in nature. The project does not have the legal status of a corporate body like the Euregions. The partners have reservations about formalising cooperation.

The network implements different projects at the same time. Some are area based. One project is developing a vision for the cross-border corridor between Antwerp and Rotterdam. Another area-based project focuses on cross-border coastal zone management. One non-area-based project is the joint marketing of the Rhine-Scheldt cross-border region in Asia.

Not only officials participate in the network but also people in politically positions are actively involved. Every project is lead by someone who holds a political office. For the implementation of projects, European co-financing is a target. Originally this European pot of gold at the end of the rainbow (Williams 1996) was an important motivation for parties to join the network. In practice, the role of European money for the Rhine-Scheldt Delta cooperative association has been rather limited. The administrative burden and additional requirements that come with European subsidies cause considerable problems.

3.5 Other forms of cooperation

Common to the modes of cooperation discussed above, with the exception of the ProSes, is that their agenda is broadly defined. Apart from these broadly based forms of cooperation, there are a number of cross-border initiatives with a more restricted mission. From 1992 onwards in the zone around the cross-border channel between Ghand and Terneuzen, two area-based environmental projects have been implemented. Both projects on each side of the border were aimed at spatial restructuring industrial activities to improve environmental qualities. While it seemed logical to integrate the two different initiatives into one cross-border project, in practice these projects have been realised separately. Those aspects of the projects with a cross-border dimension, such as the realisation of cross-border infrastructure, have not got off the ground.

There is also cooperation on cross-border nature areas. In the Rhine-Scheldt Delta there are two cross-border nature reserves – 't Zwin and Zoom-Kalmthoutseheide –, for which a joint authority has been established. In one case, Zoom-Kalmthoutseheide, a corporate body has been established on the basis of the Benelux treaty for cross-border cooperation.

Besides these *single issue* cooperative schemes, there is cooperation between 27 local authorities, BENEGO *(Belgisch-Nederlands Grensoverleg).*

This project dates back to 1967 and was formalised on the basis of the Benelux treaty in 1993. Within this general local authority, cooperation on spatial planning is just one issue among many.

3.6 Relationships between the different initiatives

Initiatives have thus been developed from different angles to increase cross-border institutional capacities to influence spatial development. These initiatives are interrelated, but ties between them are not always very strong. Coherence between the border commission VlaNed and the Rhine-Scheldt Delta cooperation is probably the strongest. An important reason is the large number of officials that participate in both initiatives. A further relationship is with ProSes. The BEU is a lynchpin between these three forms of cooperation. It is noteworthy that ProSes plans make no reference to cooperation on strategic planning or any other Rhine-Scheldt cooperation product. The strategic plan provides a spatial development perspective for the cross-border region (D'Hondt & Van Huut 2005). The Euregions are the most isolated from other modes of cooperation.

Governmental integration of cross-border management of the physical environment is still rather limited.

4 Analysis: Indirect European influence

What picture emerges from this overview? Cross-border cooperation in the area of spatial planning is characterized by informality and a lack of commitment. Only small projects are implemented, with larger themes being only the subject of debate and research.

One reason for this situation is the strong bottom-up orientation of initiatives and the broad scope applied in cooperation. This leads to a fragmented use of already limited resources. The border commission VlaNed is accountable to the Benelux transnational union, but in practice its debates are strongly influenced by the members of the commission. The Euregions are funded by the EU, but the requirements give regional actors a great deal of discretion. Not least of all because regional and local governments have to match European grants out of their own pockets. The available budget is spread over many small and diverse projects. While formally the Flemish regional and Dutch national government participate in the Rhine-Scheldt Delta Cooperation, in practice regional and local governments are the most important actors.

ProSes is an exception. This project is characterised by extensive co-operation and potentially large-scale physical transformation. It differs from other projects in the strong involvement of the Flemish regional and Dutch national governments. International law and the linkage of the Scheldt river dossier to the high speed train link dossier played an important role in the work of ProSes (Meijerink 2006). International law is important because it requires Flanders and the Netherlands to reach agreement about the maintenance of the Scheldt river. The treaty of London (1839) which arranged for the separation of Belgium from the United Kingdom of the Netherlands guarantees Belgium and Flanders the right to maintain good naval access to the harbour of Antwerp. The linkage between the Scheldt and the HSL dossiers could be established only by the central governments and was needed to break the deadlock.

Noteworthy is the relatively modest role of the EU in cross-border cooperation. While INTERREG grants offer the opportunity to implement certain projects, the INTERREG circuit is relatively isolated from other areas of cooperation in the field of the physical environment. Furthermore, the present use of European money does not contribute a great deal to cross-border institutional capacity building. The role of capacity builder in the Rhine-Scheldt Delta is fulfilled by the Secretariat-General of Benelux. Moreover, institutional capacity is restricted to the social and knowledge components. Organising political power has been problematic.

The strongly bottom-up nature of cross-border cooperation and the limited influence of European grants and rules do not imply that Europe does not play a role. The influence of the EU is more indirect, operating through the European integration discourse. This discourse has several story lines. The first postulate is that the free movement of people and goods leads to cross-border spatial development, which in turn leads to the disappearance of borders. Increasing traffic flows and the development of cross-border housing markets are conceivable. While knowledge about these processes is rather limited, it is felt in border regions that a policy response to these developments is necessary.

A second postulate is that European integration is largely brought about by joining up areas that had previously been separated by national borders. This assumption gives an ideological dimension to the unification of areas across borders, i.e., as contributing to European unification. It becomes politically correct to improve cross-border cooperation under all circumstances. Criticism of projects is not politically correct, which does not mean that politicians do their utmost to make cooperation a success.

The third postulate in the European integration discourse is that territorial competition is increasing. As a result of European integration, competition between regions is supposedly growing. Border regions seek to improve their position by cooperating with neighbouring regions in other countries. This is necessary because border regions are often peripheral to the economic core areas of nation states.

The integration discourse thus leads to initiatives in cross-border cooperation. More direct European involvement could contribute more powerful cooperation and capacity building. It requires a different European policy. In brief, present European policies lead to small-scale, concrete projects. EU policy should enable and encourage large-scale, longer lasting projects, such as ProSes, that can truly perform a strategic role at the border region level. Such projects are far out of reach under the present INTERREG programme. One reason is that the programme has a horizon of only 7 years. The impact of large strategic projects would not only affect spatial developments, but also cross-border governmental relations. These strategic projects need intensive cooperation, which would lead to more intensive mutual learning.

Furthermore, present EU policy encourages risk-avoiding projects. The accountant mentality of EU administrators implies that governments are not prepared to run the risk of not reaching targets as defined in advance, while improvement of cross-border relationships is served by venturing into unknown territories.

5 Conclusions

What are the wider implications of this analysis of cross-border co-operation in the Rhine-Scheldt Delta? First of all, it is noteworthy that the most far-reaching initiative in the region – ProSes – is a clear combination of top-down and bottom-up influence. This suggests that a context created by international law and bilateral agreements between central governments, contributes to close cooperation at the cross-border regional level.

Second, the present system of INTERREG funding does not contribute to regional cross-border capacity building. The EU induced initiatives are implemented in relative isolation.

Third, the existence of a neutral facilitator of cross-border cooperation – such as the BEU – is a great advantage that actors in the Flemish-Dutch region have at their disposal. It could be worth while for other countries to establish a joint bureau for the facilitation of cross-border cooperation.

References

BEU (= Benelux Economic Union) (1997) Ruimte voor samenwerking: Benelux Atlas [Room for cooperation: Benelux Atlas]. Benelux Economic Union, Brussels

BEU (= Benelux Economic Union) (2005) Benelux Almanak Grensoverschrijdende Samenwerking [Benelux Almanac Cross-border cooperation]. Benelux Economische Unie, Brussels

D'hondt F, van Huut H (2005) De Scheldemond kan weer lachen [The mouth of the Scheldt can laugh again]. Plandag, Amsterdam

De Vries J (2002a) Het vervagen van staatsgrenzen: De ervaringen in de Rijn-Schelde Delta [The vanishing of state borders. The experience in the Rhine-Scheldt Delta]. Agora 2, 7–10

De Vries J (2002b) Grenzen verkend. Internationalisering van de ruimtelijke planning in de Benelux [The exploration of borders. Internationalisation of spatial planning in Benelux] (PhD-thesis University of Amsterdam). DUP Science, Delft

De Vries J, Romein A, Hiethaar S, Zonneveld W, Albrechts S, Coppens T, Verachtert K (2001) Megacorridor Flemish Diamond – Randstad. OTB Delft University of Technology and ISRO Catholic University of Leuven, Delft/Leuven

Hassink R, Lagendijk A (2001) The dilemmas of interregional institutional learning. Environment and Planning C, Government and Policy: 65–84

Healey P (1997) Collaborative Planning: Shaping Places in Fragmented Societies. MacMillan, London

Knippenberg H (2004) The Maas-Rhine Euroregion: A Laboratory for European Integration? Geopolitics 9: 608-626

Martinez O J (1994) The dynamics of border interaction: New approached to border analysis. In: Schofield C H (ed) Global Bounderies. Routledge, London, New York, 1-15

Meijerink S (2006) Explaining continuity and change in international policies: Issue linkage, venue change, and learning on policies for the river Scheldt estuary. Environment and Planning A. (to be published)

Perkmann M. (1999), Building Governance Institutions Across European Borders. Regional Studies: 657-667.

Romein A, de Vries J, Albrechts L, Coppens T (2001) Policy Report on the Megacorridor Randstad – Flemish Diamond. OTB Delft University of Technology and ISRO Catholic University of Leuven, Delft, Leuven

Ruys M. (1996), Achter de maskerade. Over macht, schijnmacht en onmacht [Behind the mascerate. About power, the suggestion of power and powerlessness]. Uitgeverij Pelckmans, Kapellen

Social capital and other main influences on governance processes in cross-border micro-regions

The case of the Austrian-German Euregio 'Via Salina'

Sonja Deppisch

Dresden

1 Introduction

As integration proceeds within the European Union, the nature of internal borders is changing and border regions, too, are changing. Cross-border co-operation among different actors is an asset in transboundary sustainable development.

This chapter focuses on co-operation in cross-border regions funded by the European Commissions Community Initiative INTERREG, particularly strand A for financing cross-border institutions and single projects. While cross-border regions – often referred to as Euregios – emerged at the outset of European Integration, they flourished with the introduction of INTERREG (Perkmann 2003). Within these cross-border regions, local communities co-operate with their counterparts across the border. The term cross-border micro-region is used for this type of socially constructed regions, since Euregio is not a standard term (Conrad 2003: 111; Perkmann 2003: 159).

The aim of this paper is to explain hypothetically which main factors influence governance processes in cross-border micro-regions. It also investigates whether these micro-regions are only a response to INTERREG. This would mean that they merely implement the requirements to obtain funding. Or is INTERREG the incentive and these cross-border regions aim to govern their regional development? Are these regions reactive or also proactive? And what factors tip the balance between these different kinds of behaviour?

These questions were applied to a specific case: the Austrian-Bavarian Euregio 'Via Salina'. Interviews were held between 2004 and 2006 with representatives of the Euregio's members and external experts from subnational authorities and academia. Internal documents, press articles and websites were also analysed.

The case study is confronted with theoretical reflections on governance processes in cross-border micro-regions based on the theoretic approach of Actor Centred Institutionalism (Mayntz & Scharpf 1995a), the discussion of regional governance among German speaking scholars (Benz & Fürst 2003a; Benz & Fürst 2003b; Pütz 2004; Fürst 2005; Fürst et al. 2005), the concept of social capital (Coleman 1991; Putnam 1993) and on existing research on cross-border co-operation (e.g. Liberda 1996; Miosga 1999; Blatter 2000; Kramsch 2001; Gualini 2003; Perkmann 2003).

2 Regional governance and the concept of social capital as theoretical frame

Before presenting the leading assumptions, the theoretical basis underlying them will be described. For this purpose the above theoretic approaches are combined.

On the one hand there are the two analytical approaches Actor-Centred Institutionalism (ACI) and Regional Governance, with the latter using the main parameters of the former to analyse regional co-operation processes. The parameters used are the following: institutional context, actors and their orientations, situation, and, finally, the constellation of actors and their interactions. The starting point for this study is the assumption that political decisions or social phenomena are the result of interactions among actors behaving intentionally (Mayntz & Scharpf 1995; Scharpf 2000). The institutional context influences and structures the interactions and their results without determining them (Mayntz & Scharpf 1995: 54 f.; Scharpf 2000: 78 f.). Actors can act within and shape this context.

The regional governance discussion focuses on governance processes at the regional level relating to spatial development (Botzem 2002: 18). Going further than the state-centred debate on changes in government and decentralization (cf. Benz et al. 1999), it attributes an important role to regional networks, regional co-operation and societal governance, as well as to regional development and competitiveness. Not only governmental actors but also economic actors and civil society are considered. ACI allows their different logics of action to be integrated and analysis of other forms of interaction than hierarchical decisions (e.g. Benz & Fürst 2003a, Pütz 2004).

The specific characteristics of regional governance processes include:

- Horizontal and vertical co-operation among actors: horizontal among governmental, economic and civil society actors (Fürst 2003: 443); vertical between the local, regional, subnational, national and supranational levels in the context of European multi-level governance (Benz 2001: 57 f.).
- Combination of modes of interaction (Benz 2001: 57 f.; Benz & Fürst 2003a: 25): The institutional setting is characterized by commonly defined rules on decisions, conflicts, internal functions and cost-benefit distribution and by weak ties based on communication, trust and social norms like fairness and reciprocity as well as commitments. In consequence, negotiations are the most common form of interaction.
- Dynamic development: first, a dynamic that stems from tensions between the independent existence of cooperation and the required political control (Fürst 2001: 378). Second, cooperation itself has to evolve over time – either it leads to further institutionalisation or ceases after the initial tasks have been performed (Benz 2001: 58; Knieling 2003; Benz & Fürst 2003a).

As an analytical concept, regional governance takes these characteristics into account and focuses on regional and process-related aspects of co-operation. Because of its theoretical insufficiency in explaining regional performance, it has to be combined with other theories or research frameworks (Benz 2001: 66). ACI is often chosen as a research framework, providing the analysing criteria and main assumptions.

One the other hand, the concept of social capital as part of the social theory of Coleman (1991) provides the theoretical background to the case study. This concept was chosen because it furnishes the theoretical concept for weak forms of governance such as regional governance. Following Putnam (1993: 83 ff., 174 f.), existing social capital plays an important role in the performance of regions. The literature on regional governance points to the varying capacity of regions to build social capital (Paraskevopoulos 2001: 256; Benz & Fürst 2003b: 202). Combining different theoretical approaches is plausible because both ACI and Coleman's social theory are based on rational choice assumptions and consider individual as well as collective actors at different levels (Coleman 1991; Mayntz & Scharpf 1995; Scharpf 2000).

Social capital is generally understood as a resource of individual or collective actors for realizing certain aims (Coleman 1991 in Jans 2003: 5).

Social capital is produced by social interactions and relations. In contrast to other forms of capital, it can not be activated by a single actor but lies within the relational structures among several (at least two) actors (Coleman 1991: 409 ff.). It must thus be activated jointly.

For an overview of definitions of social capital see, for example Haug (1997) or Jans (2003). Within the given thematic context the concept of Coleman was chosen as it provides a substantial theoretical ground. Furthermore, the works of Putnam (1993) and Grix & Knowles (2003) are relevant as they apply the notion of social capital to regional or even – in the latter case – to cross-border contexts. Putnam stresses the importance of existing social capital for the performance of new regional institutions.

By confronting the theoretical parameters and concepts with research literature on cross-border co-operation, the following criteria and assumptions were developed. Before undertaking the case study, preliminary investigations were conducted on cross-border micro-regions on the Austro-German border. The results of these analyses were integrated into the final criteria and assumptions.

3 Leading assumptions on cross-border governance

First, the level of action within the cross-border micro-region is analysed. The context of European Union multi-level governance is taken into account. It implies that major contextual conditions are structured and influenced by other levels above the cross-border micro-region. The decisive criterion, however, is that individual cross-border regions are not only reactive but also proactive (cf. Fürst 2005).

Even though INTERREG is a supranational attempt to govern cross-border cooperation (cf. Miosga 1999), cross-border regions can use it to realize their own aims in regional development. This goes beyond merely implementing funding requirements. Cross-border cooperation in this respect includes more than the mere cross-border coordination of actors, namely:

- Building stable structures capable of making decisions and taking action (e.g. Fürst et al. 2005: 331).
- Developing a cross-border understanding of the cooperation process covering a wide range of thematic fields relevant to regional development (e.g. Perkmann 2003: 159 f.).
- Producing external and internal effects affecting the standing and importance attributed to the cross-border regions.

Secondly, the major factors influencing cross-border governance are considered. They can be grouped under situation, actors, existing social capital, internal institutional context, cooperation process, and external institutional context.

Situation consists of three aspects:

- topographic structure, with particular focus on cross-border barriers and on centres of population with cross-border relevance;
- shared interests and similar or even common cross-border problems regarding, for instance, the economic situation or ecological interdependencies (Van der Veen 1993: 90; Lezzi 1994: 192; Götschel 2004: 86);
- political opportunity structures regarding external interests in cross-border cooperation (Thormählen 2004: 124), e.g., funding possibilities and paradigms (cf. Blatter 2000).

The case study examines how favourable the situation is for cross-border cooperation.

Actors have to be analysed with regard to interests and orientations as well as cost-benefit appraisal and problem perception. These aspects influence actors' overall willingness to engage in cooperation. Local political and administrative actors predominate in cross-border micro-regions They usually adopt an egoistic stance centred on the interests of their own community.

The actor constellation has two aspects:

- the presence of personal difficulties among the participating actors and
- the presence of key actors who have played an important political or economic role before or during the cooperation process.

Such key actors can be important as process drivers, power players, or professional experts. Within cross-border co-operation, actors perform under difficult conditions, since institutional asymmetries, differences in language and culture, and deficient information about the neighbours lead to uncertainty. This makes key actors even more important: They have to mediate among different actors and motivate them at the beginning of the process when the anticipated costs are high and concrete benefits low. The process manager, in particular, is vital in this initial phase (Brenner 1993; Pfeiffer 2000; Thormählen 2004).

Existing social capital rooted in cooperation among localities - whether across borders or confined to the national territory – facilitates the co-operation process: local actors are already experienced in cooperation and may to some extent have established relationships based on trust (ARL 1998: 55). They are accordingly not confronted with a new and unknown mode of interaction and unknown counterparts that could evoke uncertainty (Pfeiffer 2000: 160 ff.). Grix & Knowles (2003: 10) also stress the importance of social capital that exists only on one side of the border. Disputed is the role of a cross-border sense of togetherness. Some scholars deny it any role at all while others highlight its importance in cross-border co-operation (e.g., Liberda 1996: 98; Leresche & Saez 2002: 90 ff.; Perkmann 2002: 108).

The *internal institutional context* encompasses process management, leadership and thematic work. These three functions and general procedures are considered essential to ensure stability and conflict resolution (Fürst 2003: 445). Independent process management is considered more effective than assigning the function to one of the participating actors (ARL 1998: 3, 56). However, the ideal level of institutionalization is a controversial issue (Benz & Fürst 2003a: 50 f.): Too strong institutionalization may hinder innovation as well as trustful and flexible co-operation. It also makes it more difficult to establish a transboundary sense of togetherness. On the other hand, the participating political and administrative actors need relative formal structures to legitimate their involvement. Besides, such structures allow trust to be placed in an institution and not only in individual actors. The level of institutionalization appropriate for cross-border co-operation is still a matter of dispute (cf. Miosga 1999: 175), even though a minimum of institutionalisation is regarded as prerequisite for the capacity to act jointly across the border (Thormählen 2004: 126). Existing cross-border institutions exhibit many different forms of juridical liability (Wiechmann 2003: 181 f.).

When it comes to the *cooperation process,* it is important to take account of process management and social capital formation among members of the cross-border micro-region (Benz & Fürst 2003b: 191 ff.). Management has to motivate actors, to ensure the functioning of formal structures, and to avoid interference. The management of cross-border co-operation – as opposed to cooperation within a country – requires sound ability to overcome the barrier effects of the border, to mediate among different partners and to promote the benefits of cooperation (Benz u. Fürst 2003b: 197). Social capital is deemed to play a crucial role in cross-border cooperation because trust and social relations among actors are considered to overcome difficulties and uncertainties in cross-border co-operation (Grix 2001, Grix & Knowles 2003, Klein-Hitpaß et al. 2006).

The *external institutional context causes uncertainties*. Originating from different countries, cooperating actors are confronted with many asymmetries and differences, e.g., in terms of language, culture, legislation, administration, political organisation, competencies, and governance traditions (Thormählen 2004: 123). The more different the national systems are, the more difficult cooperation will be (Pfeiffer 2000: 162 f.; Kramsch 2001: 29), because differences produce uncertainty about the potential partners for co-operation and their competencies. The legal conditions for building cross-border institutions are also important aspects of the external context (Conrad 2003: 113). Furthermore there might be competition with other institutions or administrative bodies who have already established platforms for cross-border co-operation of their own and feel threatened.

Social capital is important for cross-border co-operation because it can help overcome uncertainty among actors. Both transboundary social capital and social capital on either side of the border is needed at the beginning of the process: it motivates experienced actors to take part in or even initiate cross-border cooperation. Later it is more important that the actors who are already involved manage to establish trustful relations with each other.

Even though the focus of this article is on social capital, the other influences on cross-border governance have been introduced to avoid taking too narrow a perspective and hence risking false conclusions. The role of situation is considered to be particularly important at the beginning of the process. Potentially threatening common problems and financial incentives can be especially motivating. Many authors attribute INTERREG an important or even the most important role in the establishment of cross-border micro-regions (e.g., Blatter 2000; Perkmann 2003: 165 ff.; Danielzyk et al. 2004: 79; Herrmann & Schack 2004).

But situation becomes relevant only through actors' interests and orientations. It can bring increase the probability of cross-border co-operation but actors play the more decisive role. Existing social capital among local actors is considered to have a facilitating influence on actors' orientations towards cross-border cooperation.

The social capital that exists before the cooperation process begins is regarded as an independent influence on actors. Social generated in the course of the cooperation process is assumed to be an intervening factor influencing the outcome of the cooperation process. It is itself influenced by the external institutional context, the internal context, and actors' abilities, the actor constellation and the actors' interactions.

The external context shapes actors' competencies and hence their orientations, i.e., whether they see possibilities for acting across the border or not. It also influences the internal institutional context, as the legal form chosen depends also on the opportunities given by law. Although this is of the highest relevance in the initial phase of cooperation, the external context is nevertheless also relevant in the course of co-operation processes: then the main influencing factors are asymmetries and socio-cultural aspects. Similar competencies, structures, systems, administrative decision processes, ways of thinking and acting, as well as the same language facilitate cross-border activities and make the behaviour of an actor's counterparts from the other side of the border more comprehensible.

The role of internal structures has already been discussed. Most important is the capability of management to enhance actor motivation and the generation of social capital. This is necessary because individual actors are not interested in forming it strategically. The concrete benefits of social capital are difficult to discern for individual actors (Coleman 1991: 410 ff.). It is therefore up to management to ensure that it is formed. The moderation of interaction, mediation of conflicts and constant motivation require a highly skilled process manager.

Social capital is not only a by-product of cooperation but also affects cooperation itself. Actor preferences and interests are influenced; interaction orientations shift from egoism to solidarity. It accordingly has an important influence on regional mobilisation for action (Paraskevopoulos 2001: 256). Analysing cross-border micro-regions therefore means focusing on the abilities of the given actor constellation and management to enhance the building of new, group-related social capital. This social capital has to be communicated and maximized through cross-border co-operation (Grix & Knowles 2003: 162 f.).

4 The case of the Euregio 'Via Salina'

This cross-border micro-region was founded in 1997, two years after Austria's accession to the EU. It straddles the border between Austria and Germany and includes parts of the states *of* Bavaria, Tyrol and Vorarlberg (see fig. 1). A total of 124 local authorities are involved, as well as the three Bavarian counties of *Oberallgäu, Ostallgäu,* and *Lindau* and other organisations such as chambers of commerce or tourism networks. The majority of members are Bavarian. Austrian members are local authorities in the states of Tyrol and Vorarlberg. The cross-border micro-region consists of three national associations: the Bavarian *Regio Allgäu*, the Tyrolean regional association *REA Außerfern* and *Regio Kleinwalsertal/Bregenzerwald,* which unites the members from the state of Vorarlberg.

The Euregio 'Via Salina' is highly reactive because it focuses mainly on the funding provided by INTERREG. The cross-border region was established on local initiative. No integrative approach was adopted nor common aims or cooperative issues defined. According to external experts, the external effects of the Euregio 'Via Salina' (e.g., perception at other political levels through lobbying etc.) are weak. The region was founded and common structures were established, but they mainly serve to acquire external funds.

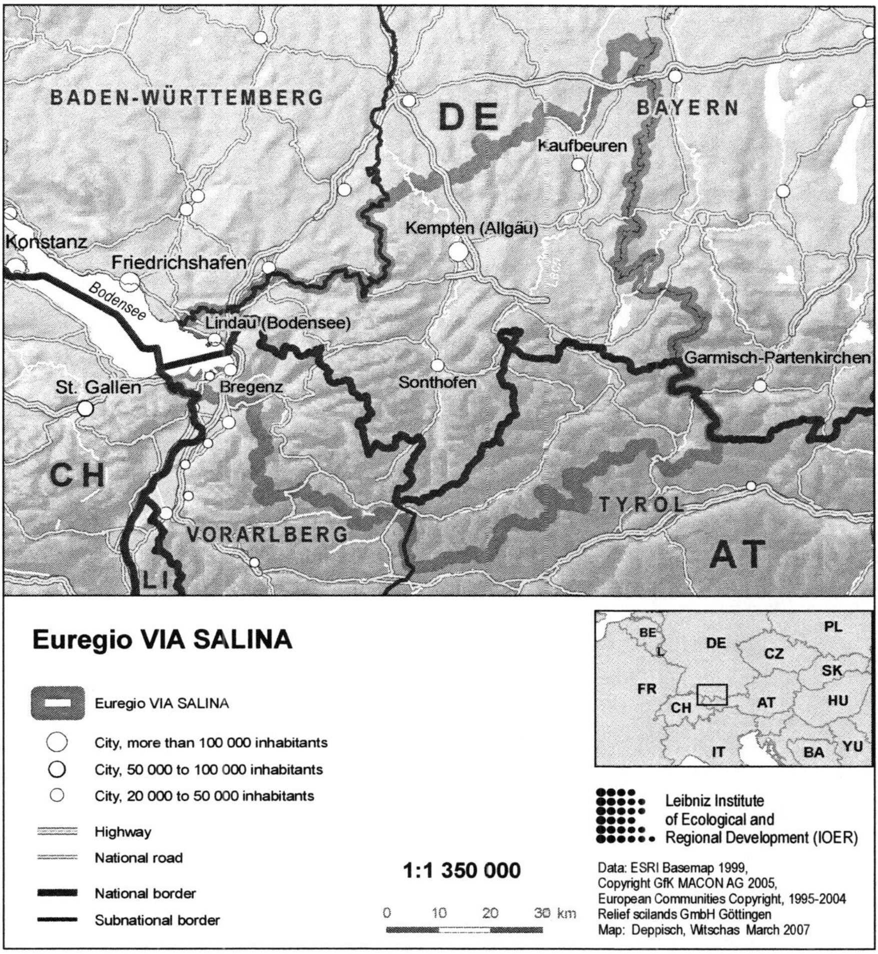

Figure 1. The Euregio 'Via Salina'

As far as *situation* is concerned, topographical connections between some Austrian areas and neighbouring German areas are better than with central Tyrol or Vorarlberg. There are even two Austrian enclaves on German territory, Kleinwalsertal and Jungholz. But in other areas, mountain ridges form barriers and no centre of population on either side of the border attracts shoppers or commuters from the other side. No urgent common problems are perceived apart from the need to overcome administrative barriers for the enclaves.

Within the third INTERREG period from 2000 to 2006 – INTEREG III A – Vorarlberg took part in the formal Austrian-Bavarian INTERREG structures but was not financially involved. Tyrol and Bavaria were members of the programme structures and provided financial input. Projects had to fulfil minimal standards of cross-border co-operation to be eligible for INTERREG funding within the Austrian-Bavarian programme. Decisions are taken by the steering committee, which includes not only representatives of the participating states but also one representative from each of the six Austrian-Bavarian Euregios (Land Oberösterreich 2003: 7 f.). The INTERREG III A Austria-Bavaria programme also includes a minor project fund. The Bavarian Euregio agency can autonomously approve projects with a budget of under € 25,000 while the Austrian neighbours have no such possibility. There is not yet a common Austrian-Bavarian clearing house, so that financial regulations differ from state to state in the two countries.

As far as relations among the states are concerned, Tyrol and Bavaria traditionally have strong ties while relations between Vorarlberg and Bavaria are less intense. The cross-border micro-regions are supported by the state governments, even though in Bavaria internal regional policy appears to take precedence and cross-border cooperation does not rank high on the political agenda.

As regards *actors,* one high-level public official - the head of the Bavarian county *Oberallgäu* is the dominant power player and process driver. The office of the Euregio 'Via Salina' is integrated into the county. This provokes scepticism among some other key actors, who keep aloof of the process. The office is not in charge of process management. Most actors, particularly key players, focus primarily on funding. A special commitment to the cross-border micro-region was not in evidence.

Existing social capital has been formed partly through regional cooperation in Tyrol. Two of the three Bavarian counties (*Landkreis Oberallgäu* and *Landkreis Ostallgäu*) traditionally compete.

As for cross-border relations, there are strong ties between individual local authorities and between smaller areas of the cross-border region. The Tyrolean area and the enclaves are historically orientated towards their German neighbours because of the topographic situation. Moreover, the two sides of the border have common cultural roots, as it traverses the Alemannic area of settlement. This explains the apparent sense of togetherness in the population.

Internal structures, including the presidency, the office and the general assembly, have been relatively stable. There are no committees to deal with substantive issues. The office assumes no management functions in the co-operation process. Instead it focuses on INTERREG-related tasks. What is more, it does not operate as a common cross-border institution. Instead, it is dominated by the Bavarian side since it is integrated into the administration of one of the Bavarian member counties. This implies dependency.

But the functions of the office are also limited due to a lack of commitment among participating entities: they are just willing to finance a part-time employment. Nor is there much willingness to invest time. Overall costs are shared as follows: Regio Allgäu (Bavaria) 85%, REA Außerfern (Tyrol) 10%, and Regio Kleinwalsertal/Bregenzerwald 5%.

Thus the role of the office in the *process* is limited. Compared with the initial phase of cross-border co-operation, even public relations activities have diminished. Nobody is responsible for motivating actors and strengthening ties among participants because there is no cross-border process management.

Furthermore, competition between two Bavarian counties is hard to overcome. Almost no transboundary social capital has been added to that existing among the mayors of neighbouring local authorities. Limited to a few political actors, contacts became more intensive through informal cooperation. To some extent, cultural co-operation has also intensified. But no broad and stable region-wide cooperation process has emerged through the establishment of the cross-border micro-region.

The *external institutional context* influences the cross-border micro-region in different ways. On the one hand conditions for cooperation are good since actors share a common language and cultural background. Local authority competencies are also relatively strong in both countries, since the national constitutions guarantee local self-government. Even though there are differences in administrative structures at the local level – there is no Austrian equivalent of the German county *[Landkreis]*, this does not pose a problem for cooperation. However, legislative asymmetries in various fields do not facilitate matters. Moreover, Vorarlberg's failure to contribute financially and different modalities for approving small projects in Tyrol and Bavaria provoke uncertainty. Furthermore cross-border co-operation in rural development financed by the European Community Initiative Leader appears to be competing with Euregio 'Via Salina' processes, which has failed to integrate the activities in this field. The Tyrolean association even seems to rely more on this cross-border co-operation.

5 Conclusions

How is the low level of action in the Euregio 'Via Salina' to be explained? – Even though the topographical situation appears to offer potential, it has provided no positive impact. Other assumptions concerning the situation can be confirmed: no population centre attracts cross-border activities, and no impetus is provided by common urgent problems. INTERREG plays a major role; actors are mainly interested in funding. The office staffs also see their main field of action in the implementation of INTERREG requirements. This empirical finding is in line with Perkmann's conclusion (1999: 663 f.) that local cross-border networks play an important role in delivering European Commission INTERREG policies, although it is questionable whether the Euregio 'Via Salina' contributes to the original aims of INTERREG III A at all.

Social capital is constituted by single ties, but the difficult and competitive relations between the two Bavarian counties appears to dominate cross-border cooperation. According to the interviews conducted, this is due not mainly to the constellation of actors but to the traditionally difficult relationship between theses two counties. The stock of supportive cross-border connections was not increased. This is an argument in favour of the thesis that social capital on either side of the border is also important for the cooperation process as a whole. Because competition and difficult relations reinforce existing barriers, this supports assumptions about existing social capital: existing social capital has an impact not only during the initial phase of cooperation but throughout the process. It even influences the final outcomes of cooperation.

The benefits of cooperation were communicated neither to participants nor to the broader public. This is in the responsibility of key actors, whose commitment and orientation towards an active cross-border micro-region was lacking. Obviously they are primarily interested in acquiring funding and improving their personal political standing through symbolic cross-border activities and new positions within the internal structures, e.g., in the presidency.

Furthermore, the small and dependent office is incapable of driving co-operation. It cannot induce actors to intensify cooperation or construct a network with stronger ties. This weakness strongly influences the cooperation process and its final outcomes. But the independence and room for manoeuvre of the office itself is affected by the small budget and of its integration into the administrative structures of a partisan Bavarian county. Scepticism is also aroused among participants by the fact that the leadership and office are in one hand. The internal context is thus not conducive to cross-border reliability. A transboundary internal structure devoted to an overall cross-border interest is lacking.

The fact that there are no thematic working groups or the like shows the lack of commitment among members.

The higher number of Bavarian actors and the continuity of the presidency since the establishment of the micro-region evoke an image of imbalance or even dominance.

An overall cross-border cooperation process building new and group-specific social capital has not nearly been achieved. No measures whatsoever to stimulate social capital formation have been taken. There is neither incentive for potential actors to participate nor a concrete added value besides the new symbolic cross-border cooperation. This proceeds in soft fields like culture, where no conflicts are to be expected and no strategic input is necessary. The cross-border micro-region 'Via Salina' seems to focus on funding and reputation.

The most striking aspect is this weak result, even though the external institutional context does produce less uncertainty than expected in cross-border cooperation. The decisive factors appear to be a lack of interest and orientation on the part of actors, insufficient social capital, and difficult relations on the Bavarian side.

The following hypotheses can be formulated with regard to social capital:

- Not only previously existing cross-border social capital, but also social capital on either side of the border has an important influence on cross-border governance processes.
- If there is negative social capital on one side of the border– i.e., tensions and severe competition among actors expected to cooperate – the cross-border co-operation process faces serious difficulties.
- Cooperation in a cross-border region does not necessarily alter prevailing competitive attitudes among participating actors. If competition remains their main motivation for cooperation, they will not be ready to install a strong organisational structure for cooperation. This has been illustrated by the dependent and poorly funded office in the case study which was an indicator for the lacking interest in real cooperation.

It can be concluded that it is very difficult to build new social capital among members of a cross-border micro-region under conditions such as those pertaining in the Euregio 'Via Salina'.

References

ARL (= Akademie für Raumforschung und Landesplanung) (1998) Interkommunale und regionale Kooperation - Variablen ihrer Funktionsfähigkeit [Intraregional co-operation - variables to be in working order]. Verlag der ARL, Hannover

Benz A (2001) Vom Stadt-Umland-Verband zu "regional governance" in Stadtregionen [Towards regional governance in city regions]. Deutsche Zeitschrift für Kommunalwissenschaften 40, 55–71

Benz A (2003) Regional Governance mit organisatorischem Kern. Das Beispiel der Region Stuttgart [Regional governance with a organisational centre. The example of region Stuttgart]. Informationen zur Raumentwicklung 8/9, 505–512

Benz A, Fürst D (2003a) Region – "Regional Governance" – Regionalentwicklung [Region – regional governance – regional development]. In: Adamaschek B, Pröhl M (eds) Regionen erfolgreich steuern. Regional Governance – von der kommunalen zur regionalen Strategie [Successful Regional Governance – from communal towards regional strategies], Verlag Bertelsmann Stiftung, Gütersloh, 11–66

Benz A, Fürst D (2003b) Erfolgsbedingungen für "Regional Governance" – Resümee [Success factors for regional governance]. In: Adamaschek B, Pröhl M (eds) Regionen erfolgreich steuern. Regional Governance – von der kommunalen zur regionalen Strategie [Successful Regional Governance – from communal towards regional strategies]. Verlag Bertelsmann Stiftung, Gütersloh, 189–211

Benz A, Fürst D, Kilper H, Rehfeld D (1999) Regionalisierung. Theorie – Praxis – Perspektiven [Regionalisation. Theory – Practise – Perspectives]. Leske + Budrich, Opladen

Blatter J (2000) Entgrenzung der Staatenwelt? Politische Institutionenbildung in grenzüberschreitenden Regionen in Europa und Nordamerika [Debordering of nation-states? Cross-border processes of institutionalisation in Europe and Northern America]. Nomos, Baden-Baden

Botzem S (2002) Governance-Ansätze in der Steuerungsdiskussion. Steuerung und Selbstregulierung unter den Bedingungen fortschreitender Internationalisierung [Governance approaches within the debate on government]. Wissenschaftszentrum Berlin für Sozialforschung, Berlin

Brenner P (1993) What Makes an INTERREGional Network Successful? In: Cappelin R, Batey PWJ (eds) Regional networks, Border Regions and European Integration, Pion, London, 239-244

Coleman JS (1991) Grundlagen der Sozialtheorie [Social theory]. Oldenbourg, München

Conrad CM (2003) Rechtliche Entwicklung der grenzüberschreitenden Zusammenarbeit von europäischen Regionen im Zeitalter der Globalisierung. Ausdruck von Denationalisierung und Neuorganisation [Juridical development of cross-border co-operation between European regions in the era of

globalisation. Expression of de-nationalisation and reorganisation]. Peter Lang, Frankfurt a. M.
Danielzyk R, Ernste H, Jung H-U (2004) Fallstudien für deutsch-niederländische Grenzräume [Case studies in German-Dutch borderlands]. In: Thormählen L (ed) Entwicklung europäischer Grenzräume bei abnehmender Bedeutung nationaler Grenzen. Deutsch-dänische und deutsch-niederländische Grenzräume im europäischen Integrationsprozess [Development of European border regions in the wake of decreasing importance of national borders. German-Danish and German-Dutch border regions in the process of European integration]. Verlag der ARL, Hannover, 78–115
Fürst D (2001) Regional governance – ein neues Paradigma der Regionalwissenschaften? [Regional governance – a new paradigm in regional science?], Raumforschung und Raumordnung 5–6, 370–380
Fürst D (2003) Steuerung auf regionaler Ebene versus Regional Governance [Government on a regional scale versus regional governance]. Informationen zur Raumentwicklung 8/9, 441–450
Fürst D (2005) Regional Governance. In: Benz A (ed) Governance – Regieren in komplexen Regelsystemen. Eine Einführung [Governance – Government in complex institutional systems. An introduction]. VS Verlag für Sozialwissenschaften, Wiesbaden, 45–64
Fürst D, Lahner M, Pollermann K (2005) Regional Governance bei Gemeinschaftsgütern des Ressourcenschutzes: das Beispiel Biosphärenreservate [Regional governance regarding the protection of ressources – the example of biosphere reserves]. Raumforschung und Raumordnung 5, 330–339
Gabbe J (2003) Grenzübergreifende Region Euregio [Cross-border region Euregio]. In: Adamaschek B, Pröhl M (eds) Regionen erfolgreich steuern. Regional Governance – von der kommunalen zur regionalen Strategie [Successful Regional Governance – from communal towards regional strategies]. Verlag Bertelsmann Stiftung, Gütersloh, 155–175
Götschel U (2004) Europa – Region – Kommune. Optimierung europäischer Mehrebenenpolitik durch die Euregio PAMINA? [Europe – Region – Local Community. Optimization of European multi-level-politics through Euregio PAMINA?]. Nomos, Baden-Baden
Grix J (2001) Towards a Theoretical Approach to the Study of Cross-Border Cooperation, Perspectives. Review of Central European Affairs 17: 5–13
Grix J, Knowles V (2003) The Euroregion and the Maximization of Social Capital: Pro Europa Viadrina. In: Anderson L, O'Dowd L, Wilson TM (eds) New borders for a changing Europe: cross-border cooperation and governance, Frank Cass, London, 154–176
Gualini E (2003) Cross-border Governance: Inventing Regions in a Trans-national Multi-level Polity. DISP 152: 43–52
Herrmann H, Schack M (2004) Fallstudien für deutsch-dänische Grenzräume [Case studies in German-Danish borderlands]. In: Thormählen L (ed) Entwicklung europäischer Grenzräume bei abnehmender Bedeutung nationaler Grenzen. Deutsch-dänische und deutsch-niederländische

Grenzräume im europäischen Integrationsprozess [Development of European border regions in the wake of decreasing importance of national borders. German-Danish and German-Dutch border regions in the process of European integration]. Verlag der ARL, Hannover, 20–77

Klein-Hitpaß K, Leibenath M, Knippschild R (2006) Vertrauen in grenzüberschreitenden Akteursnetzwerken. Erkenntnisse aus dem deutsch-polnisch-tschechischen Kooperationsprojekt ENLARGE-NET [Trust in cross-border networks of actors – the case of the German-Polish-Czech cooperation project ENLARGE-Net]. DISP 164: 59–70

Knieling J (2003) Kooperative Regionalplanung und Regional Governance: Praxisbeispiele, Theoriebezüge und Perspektiven [Co-operative regional planning and regional governance. Practical examples, theoretical references and perspectives]. Informationen zur Raumentwicklung 8/9: 463–478

Kramsch O. (2001), Navigating the Spaces of Kantian Reason: Notes on Cosmopolitical Governance within the Cross-Border Euregios of the European Union. Geopolitics 6, 27-50

Leresche JP, Saez G (2002) Political Frontier Regimes: Towards Cross-Border Governance. In: Perkmann M, Sum NL (eds) Globalization, Regionalization and Cross-border Regions. Palgrave macmillan, Houndmills, 77–99

Lezzi M (1994) Raumordnungspolitik in europäischen Grenzregionen zwischen Konkurrenz und Zusammenarbeit [Spatial planning policies in European border regions between competition and cooperation]. Philosophische Fakultät II, Universität Zürich, Zürich

Liberda E (1996) Regionalentwicklung in Grenzregionen: Eine Euregio als Regionalentwicklungsstrategie? Das Beispiel der Inn-Salzach-Euregio an der bayerisch-oberösterreichischen Grenze [Regional development in border regions: Euregio as strategy of regional development? Case study of Inn-Salzach Euregio at the Bavarian-Upper Austrian border]. Passavia, Passau

Mayntz R, Scharpf FW (1995) Der Ansatz des akteurzentrierten Institutionalismus [The approach of Actor-centred Institutionalism]. In: Mayntz R, Scharpf FW (eds) Gesellschaftliche Selbstregelung und politische Steuerung [Political self-regulation and government]. Campus, Frankfurt a. M., New York, 39–72

Miosga M (1999) Europäische Regionalpolitik in Grenzregionen. Die Umsetzung der INTERREG-Initiative am Beispiel des nordrhein-westfälisch-niederländischen Grenzraums [European Regional policy in border regions. Implementation of the Community Initiative INTERREG taking as example case studies within the North Rhine-Westphalian-Dutch borderland]. Passavia, Passau

O'Dowd L (2002) The Changing Significance of European Borders. Regional and Federal Studies 12, 13–36

Paraskevopoulos CJ (2001) Social Capital, Learning and EU Regional Policy Networks: Evidence from Greece. Government and Opposition 36, 253–279

Perkmann M (1999) Building Governance Institutions Across European Borders. Regional Studies 33, 657–667

Perkmann M (2002) The rise of the Euroregion. A bird's eye perspective on European cross-border co-operation, Department of Sociology. Lancaster University, Lancaster UK

Perkmann M (2003) Cross-border regions in Europe. Significance and drivers of regional cross-border co-operation. European Urban and Regional Studies 10, 153–171

Pfeiffer T (2000) Erfolgsbedingungen grenzüberschreitender regionaler Zusammenarbeit. [Success factors of regional cross-border co-operation]. Peter Lang, Frankfurt a. M.

Putnam RD (1993) Making Democracy Work. Civic Traditions in Modern Italy, Princeton University Press, Princeton

Pütz M (2004) Regional Governance. Theoretisch-konzeptionelle Grundlagen und eine Analyse nachhaltiger Siedlungsentwicklung in der Metropolregion München [Regional Governance. Theoretic-conceptual foundations and a case study on sustainable development of settlement structures in the metropolitan region Munich]. Oekom, München

Scharpf FW (2000) Interaktionsformen. Akteurzentrierter Institutionalismus in der Politikforschung. [Orig.: 1997 – Games Real Actors Play]. Leske + Budrich, Opladen

Thormählen L (2004) Grenzübergreifende Zusammenarbeit in europäischen Grenzräumen – eine bewertende Zusammenfassung [Summary of cross-border co-operation in European border regions]. In: Thormählen L (ed) Entwicklung europäischer Grenzräume bei abnehmender Bedeutung nationaler Grenzen. Deutsch-dänische und deutsch-niederländische Grenzräume im europäischen Integrationsprozess [Development of European border regions in the wake of decreasing importance of national borders. German-Danish and German-Dutch border regions in the process of European integration]. Verlag der ARL, Hannover, 121–130

Van der Veen A (1993) Theory and Practice of Cross-border Cooperation of Local Governments: The Case of the EUREGIO Between Germany and the Netherlands. In: Cappelin R, Batey PWJ (eds) Regional networks, Border Regions and European Integration. Pion, London, 89–95

Wiechmann T (2003) Schwieriger Sonderfall oder Modell für Europas Regionen? Zusammenfassende Thesen zu den Regionen Pamina und Euregio [Difficult and special cases or models for European regions? Summarizing theses on the regions Pamina and Euregio]. In: Adamaschek B, Pröhl M (eds) Regionen erfolgreich steuern. Regional Governance – von der kommunalen zur regionalen Strategie [Successful Regional Governance – from communal towards regional strategies]. Verlag Bertelsmann Stiftung, Gütersloh, 176–188

III Cross-border co-operation between cities and metropolitan regions

Cross-border cooperation challenges: Positioning the Vienna-Bratislava region

Matej Jaššo

Institute of Spatial Planning and Urban Design, Faculty of Architecture, Slovak Technical University, Bratislava

1 Introduction

The transformation and restructuring of European regions have been among the key topics of the social and economic discourse in recent years. European integration is an important process which, among other things, leads to a common market. The pressure of competition accordingly increases not only for private enterprises but even for regions and cities as a whole. Competition and cooperation between European regions have become prominent issues in debates among spatial planners, economists, sociologists and other experts (e.g., Giffinger 2005; Hall 2006).

Fostered by processes of globalization, EU enlargement and new impulses in the field of information technologies, regions have discovered completely new roles and positions. The national level has been continuously weakened and new developmental challenges have appeared at all levels and in many different fields. More than ever, the new situation requires unique, original and plausible profiles for each region aspiring to success in a competitive environment.

The struggle for competitive advantage has become more and more significant in development strategies and policies at various spatial levels. Regions are successively forced to compete for foreign investments in the economic field, in culture and tourism, where all the relevant actors are highly mobile and sensitive to the standards of location factors at the urban-regional level.

This competition is often heavier than market competition in commercial business structures and requires precise strategic management and marketing policy (for more theoretical perspectives cf. Kottler et al. 1994; Kozma 2006: 73). However, the positioning of European regions should be perceived as a process which is open and transparent in each of its phases, avoiding final and definitive completion, although requiring clear target orientation.

The general, basic idea of the concept of competition between regions is to create and open a profile of a region as an "attractive, unique and competitive product" (Schwandt 1997, cited in Dettmar 2001). The region is considered as a product that is strategically put on the market and which is developed for the market, whereby the word "market" as such should not be perceived in commercial terms alone. However, a massive increase in competition between regions provokes a constant search for new forms of expression and more sophisticated communication tools.

In developing the product with its particular sub-products, the following criteria should be considered as most relevant (Schwandt 1997, cited in Dettmar 2001):

- long term duration and conceptual nature,
- integrative and interdisciplinary approach,
- close links between planning and implementation,
- local needs and potentials must be taken into consideration,
- consensus and coordination of the activities, and
- flexible organisation structure and decision making mechanisms.

The paper is based on analyses of both Vienna and Bratislava and their mutual relations, which constitute the metropolitan region Vienna-Bratislava. The positioning of this region is studied with regard to three possible future scenarios: Vienna agglomeration, TwinCity concept, and CENTROPE region. Although the scenarios partly overlap and refer to different institutional backgrounds, they illustrate different paths to the future positioning of the Vienna-Bratislava region and subsequent marketing, implementation and communication activities.

The paper has five main sections. Chapter two introduces the two cities of Vienna and Bratislava. Then the development and the current situation of the Vienna-Bratislava metropolitan area, as well as the trends and challenges it faces are examined. On this basis, three scenarios or projects are presented concerning the future development of this Central European region (chapter 4). Finally, conclusions are drawn, including critical assessment of the cross-border cooperation initiatives in the Vienna-Bratislava metropolitan region (chapter 5).

2 Unequal partners

2.1 The city of Vienna

Vienna is capital of the Federal Republic of Austria and a separate state of the federation (Land Wien). It covers an area of 414 km^2 and has a population of 1.65 million. Thus, Vienna is home to 20% of the Austrian population and accounts for 27% of the respective national GDP.

Located on the site of an old Roman settlement (Vindobona), Vienna is a vibrant metropolis with a rich cultural, historical and architectural heritage. The old city centre with its many precious historical architectural elements ranging from medieval to modern buildings, Vienna´s unparalleled cultural landscape represented by the Museum of the History of Arts, the Albertina and the museum quarter, as well as the modern complex of the UNO City are the most prominent examples worth noting (Hofmann 2004).

Vienna has always enjoyed the image and prestige of a highly respectable centre of culture, education and science. The principal goal in this field, embodied in the Strategy Plan of 2004, is to keep, accent and further develop this reputation. Cooperation between universities, research institutes, and commercial business organisations is to be strengthened and intensified. The cultural policy of the municipality is convincingly aimed at fostering the open-minded cultural climate that has always been typical of the city's cultural milieu. Creativity and experimental work are systematically utilised as impulses for urban development under the heading "creative industries" (Magistrat der Stadt Wien 2004: 13–17).

Vienna is a colourful mosaic of various cultural influences, mentalities, and ways of life. Present-day Vienna is striving to overcome its old, clichés image, for example as the "city of the waltz". In 1979 the city received the status as 3rd UN City after New York and Geneva and became a synonym for "gateway to Eastern Europe".

Since the political changes in the late 1980s, Vienna has adopted several new roles. The metropolis, located for decades of the periphery of Western Europe's political system, has rapidly developed into the principal metropolis of Central Europe. The Strategy Plan (Magistrat der Stadt Wien 2004) embodies the developmental priorities and principles based upon the city's principal values, namely the notions of sustainability, global responsibility and future-oriented action. The strategic vision ("Leitbild") includes regional cooperation. Vienna aspires to leadership in the process of competition and cooperation between European cities and regions on the basis of innovative, sustainable and flexible regional policy (Magistrat der Stadt Wien 2005).

2.2 The city of Bratislava

Bratislava is the capital, as well as the administrative and economic centre of the Slovak Republic. In the context of economic and political relations, its location beyond the Eastern fringe of the old EU-15 is a specific advantage of strategic importance. Bratislava has been given the opportunity to play a unique and versatile role of a city at the interface between old and new EU members. The outstanding potential of Bratislava's location could not be utilised until 1989. Owing to intensified social and economic contacts with its highly developed and economic prosperous neighbour Vienna, the regional relations of Bratislava have gained new dimensions. The proximity of Vienna - the distance is less than 60 km - facilitates both emerging new agglomeration tendencies and cross-border cooperation. This may lead to the rise of a new urban region of global importance, spanning the borders of three or four countries, because Hungary and the Czech Republic are close by, too.

In a 1993 comparative assessment of 471 European regions, the Vienna-Bratislava-Györ region was judged Europe's most promising economic area (Finka & Zigrai 2005). While the population of Bratislava – 428,672 inhabitants (Hrdina 2002a: 4) – accounts for only 8.4% of the national population, it generates approximately one-third of gross domestic product (GDP).

Most foreign direct investment in Slovakia has been concentrated in and around the city. Its share of investment has reached 55%, and the city is a driving force for economic activity throughout the country. With an unemployment rate only a quarter of the Slovak average, Bratislava has the lowest unemployment in the country. The favourable economic environment of the city is indicated by the high purchasing power, which – relative to the average wage – is 50% above the Slovak average.

Bratislava's exceptional economic status was also confirmed by a recent study comparing GDP per capita in 89 regions of the new EU Member States, then still accession candidates. The study revealed that, in terms of purchasing power parity, the Bratislava region's GDP equalled 105% of the EU average even in 1999. This rate is 3–4 times higher than the average for the rest of Slovakia's regions. The extremely steep increase in spatial polarisation among Slovakian regions accelerated still further, and regional disparities are among the most difficult challenges facing spatial development in the country (Hrdina 2002a: 5).

Despite favourable geopolitical and economic conditions, Bratislava still has to compensate a number of disadvantages. The city is struggling with

- a rather fuzzy image,
- a low degree of integrity in communication tools and methods,

- a lack of modern approaches regarding cultural heritage propagation and marketing management, as well as
- insufficient participation by business organisations in communicating the "product" Bratislava and its particular traits.

Marketing communication has been rather hectic and superficial, although the city has striven to apply modern strategic city marketing and management methods and approaches, such as branding and corporate identity.

Strengthening the role of Bratislava as a medium-sized European metropolis and new trends in tourism such as congress tourism, incentives tourism and cross-border cooperation regarding city events are likely to be the greatest challenges in the near future.

3 Vienna-Bratislava metropolitan region

3.1 Historical development

The Vienna-Bratislava region is situated at one of the principal historical, cultural and infrastructural cross-roads of Europe and is an integral part of numerous sectoral networks. In this area the problems and opportunities involved in dismantling the "iron curtain" have been glaringly manifest. Two interlinked trends and their beneficial effects on development and growth in a unified Europe are apparent - the decreasing importance of national barriers with the related integration of national, regional and local economies, and, on the other hand, the emergence of new development poles in the form of functional regions that cut across administrative borders (Finka 2005).

The Vienna-Bratislava region has had strong functional ties throughout its long, close and sometimes shifting history. Periods in which the border played a minor role have alternated with eras in which the two cities belonged to different political systems (Finka 2005: 125).

Until the 19th century, Vienna and Bratislava belonged to one territorial unit – the Austrian Habsburg Monarchy with its common market and currency. Vienna was the 4th biggest city worldwide and the capital of the Austrian Monarchy with 2 million inhabitants.

At that time, Bratislava was the capital of the Hungarian part of the Empire. The city really featured many cultures and languages. Although it had a population of less than 60.000, Bratislava maintained its position as the second most important industrial city in Hungary.

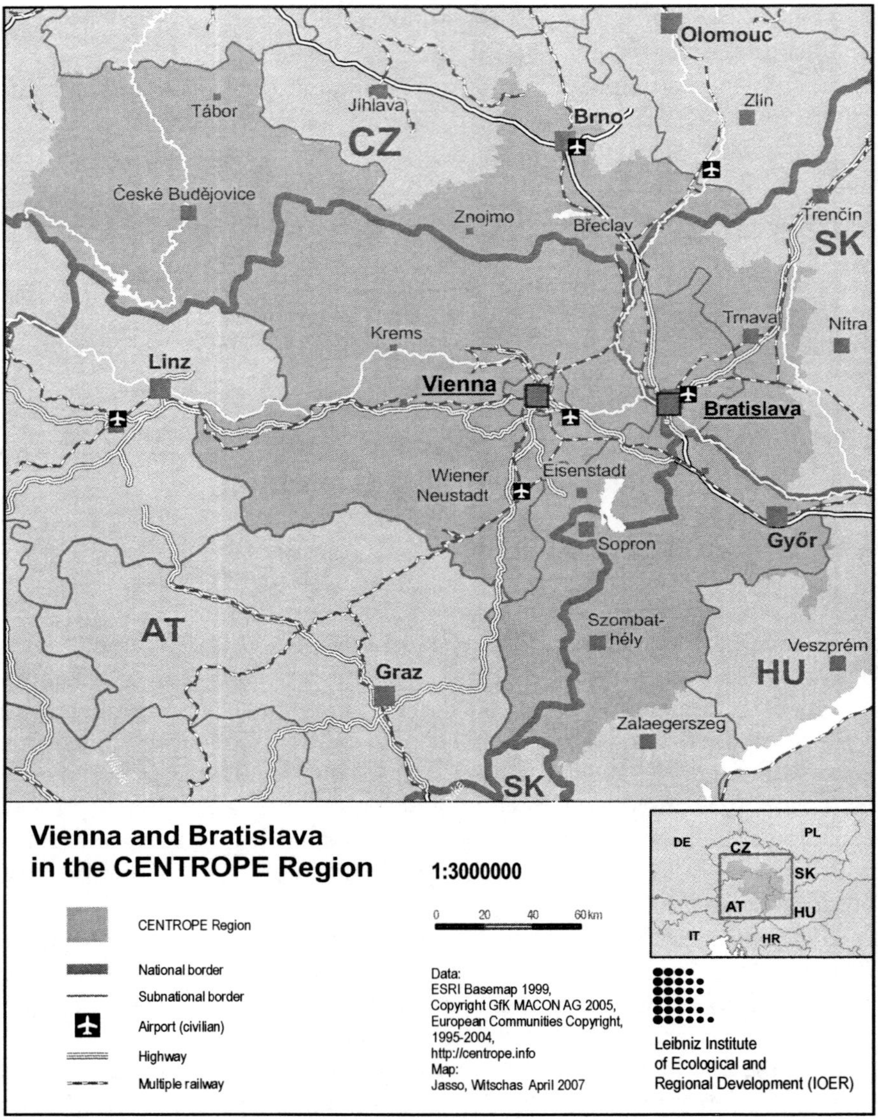

Figure 1. Bratislava-Vienna Region

In the absence of any trade, language or cultural barriers between Vienna and Bratislava, cooperation flourished in all fields. Railway and river connections were intensively utilized.

The division of the Old Monarchy into an Austrian and an Hungarian part in 1867 raised administrative barriers and strongly hampered cooperation between the two cities.

After World War II, Europe was politically divided and cooperation ceased. Vienna and Bratislava merely co-existed without any form of institutionalized cooperation. The era of the Cold War and the division of Europe into two antagonistic blocks made this previously centrally located region very peripheral in many aspects for more than 40 years. This holds especially true for the Austrian municipalities which had no contact with Bratislava. The division almost completely dissolved transboundary industrial, cultural and communication networks.

This situation persisted until the change of regime in the former Czechoslovakia in 1989. Political and economic changes like those taking place in all other former socialist countries completely redefined the roles and positions of both parts of the region. The relationship gained a new quality through mutual communication and feedback and through common projects which have been started in various fields since the early 1990s. However, the necessary strategic background and balance was sometimes lacking. There was no long-term strategic effort in this field. Considerable imbalances in the structure of Austrian and Slovak local authorities and government bodies retarded vital cooperation.

Several cross-border projects such as JORDES+ or the joint INTERREG III A / Phare CBC programmes have been implemented in recent years. They have focused mainly on issues like sustainable industrial development or transport infrastructure. However, an efficient transboundary policy for the Vienna-Bratislava region has not yet been entirely achieved. The identification of policy priorities and the process of developing sustainable cross-border institutions are still at an early stage. A more active approach by the key players– the municipalities of Vienna and Bratislava – seems to be urgently needed.

Economic development gained momentum from the economic transition in Slovakia and from Austria's accession to the EU in 1995. This improved the region's position in the European "competition of regions". Local economies on both sides of the border became more open and increasingly converged. Cross-border integration has been beneficial in economic, social and cultural terms for both Vienna and Bratislava:

> "Since 1995, both the Bratislava and Vienna part of the region have grown faster than their respective home countries. Moreover, most indicators show regional convergence. While nominal GDP per capita in Bratislava was less than 20% of Vienna in 1995, it approached 30% in 2002 and is estimated to be at around 50% in 2015" (Finka 2005: 126).

3.2 Current situation

Vienna and Bratislava form the most closely located pair of capitals in the world. Both cities now play prominent roles in the development of the whole region and the overall nature of cooperative relations among various actors in the region is significantly influenced by the quality of relations between Vienna and Bratislava.

National barriers began to lose their importance with the accelerating integration of national, regional and local economies in the early 1990s. The current status of the metropolitan region Vienna-Bratislava might serve as a prime example of this trend.

The fundamental functions of the Vienna-Bratislava region have been described as follows (Hrdina et al. 2002b: 99):

- to become a development pole of European significance, based on a concentration of specific human, scientific, cultural, technological and institutional potentials as well as on adequate transportation and communication interconnections to other development poles in Europe;
- to become a residential, economic and cultural centre of the upper and middle Danube line;
- to become one of the development centres in Central Europe, which has gained importance after the accession of the Visegrád countries to the EU – Czech Republic, Hungary, Poland and Slovakia;
- to become an economic, cultural and information gateway to Austria and Slovakia;
- to strengthen functional ties between the two capital cities and their less favoured suburban surroundings on the territory of the Slovak Republic, Austria and Hungary;

In fact, the bi-national region constitutes the core of an emerging bigger functional region – the central European region of Bratislava-Vienna-Brno-Gyor. It encompasses the Austrian states of Vienna, Lower Austria and Burgenland, creating the Vienna Metropolitan Region and the two Slovak regions of Bratislava and Trnava belonging to the Bratislava Metropolitan Region. The Bratislava Metropolitan Region makes up roughly one-quarter of both area and inhabitants in the Vienna – Bratislava region. (Finka 2005: 124)

This cross-border region with more than 5 million inhabitants and 2.5 million jobs is a unique spatial configuration in Central Europe. The prospects of its becoming a major cultural, intellectual, transport and knowledge pole have increased in recent years. Although the main players are the cities of Vienna and Bratislava, the synergy effects of spatial and economic development have brought new challenges and opportunities for other, more peripheral parts of the broader region such as the Austrian state of Burgenland or the Slovakian Trnava County.

The region covers a wide range of landscapes such as the Danube river basin, the Carpathian Mountains and the Pannonian lowland which create unique spatial structures apt for various forms and types of spatial development. Moreover, the diversity of the region is completed by the multiplicity of languages and cultural patterns.

Demographic development differs among core cities, sub-centres and peripheral municipalities. Suburbanization with migration to the outskirts of the metropolitan area became the dominant trend. With the increasing attractiveness of the core cities, the process of re-urbanization has begun (Hrdina 2002b: 24). Urban sprawl in the suburban space has increased while peripheral parts of the region have to face a loss of younger population and a rising average age of the remaining population. As in the region as a whole, the integration process has shifted the location of particular municipalities from peripheral to central.

One of the main reasons for economic imbalances is still disparities in prices and wage levels. The Slovakian currency was very much undervalued, with an exchange rate deviation index (ERDI) figure of 2.75 as compared to Austria (Hrdina 2002a: 6). This makes foreign investment attractive but also brings increases the risk of a brain drain. The disparity tempts investors to relocate production at a lower technological level and less skilled jobs to the Slovakian part of the region. In order to counteract this process and to attract sophisticated business activities instead of cheap production, the City of Bratislava stresses its highly qualified human resource structure as one of its principal strategic advantages.

Although the Slovakian part of the Vienna-Bratislava metropolitan region has a sectoral structure similar to the Austrian part, lower wages and lower productivity hinder the compatibility of labour markets in the two parts of the region. Labour mobility between Slovakia and Austria is surprisingly low, despite substantial income differences. This is due to a restrictive Austrian policy to protect its labour market against competition.

3.3 Trends and challenges

Globalisation and accelerating competition between European cities and regions have strongly influenced the position of both Vienna and Bratislava as well as the chances of the region as a whole. Vienna itself will face major challenges and tasks in competing with “premier league” cities (Finka & Zigrai 2005). Without effective cooperation with Bratislava as its major partner and with smaller regional partners, Vienna can hardly fulfil this task.

Deliberate, meaningful and transparent cooperation between the two cities and all regional actors will bring about the required synergy effects. It is necessary to improve links between research, development and industry.

4 Scenarios and projects for the future development of the Vienna-Bratislava metropolitan region

4.1 Vienna agglomeration

Vienna is much bigger than Bratislava - nearly three times the size in terms of population – and has more influence and power. If there was sharp and all-encompassing competition between these cities, the stronger city would prevail and retain its dominance. One-sided orientation towards Vienna has been the dominant historical pattern in this region in previous centuries. Vienna displayed and maintained its powerful political and economic position. If this pattern were to be revitalised, it would bring a "revival of old history" and relegate all other actors in the greater region to subordinated roles.

In the short run, Vienna could reap benefits from such a situation. This development would lead to the allocation of low-tech production plants to peripheral areas – and especial eastern parts – of the region and to the concentration of highly skilled labour and sophisticated functions in Vienna. As we have seen, this is already happening to some extent.

On the other hand, such a development is neither in the interest of Vienna nor of Bratislava. The Austrian workforce in Vienna would suffer significant wage cuts if the Austrian labour market was fully liberalised and opened to competition with Slovakian workers. The marginalisation of the Slovak part of the metropolitan region and of the adjacent Hungarian and Moravian regions would cause spatial conflicts such as the escalation of land-use and transport problems and social imbalances due to brain-drain. Moreover, this trend would fix the status quo of 'two players in different leagues' and would collide with the aims of social cohesion and negate a common vision.

As the negative implications of this scenario clearly outweigh the potential advantages for both sides, it was abandoned in the mid-1990s in favour of other models.

4.2 Twin city

The twin city concept aims to develop a functionally coherent region characterised by the synergic utilisation of socio-economic potential of both cities. It calls for co-ordinated activities by public sector administrative bodies, NGOs, and business enterprises in both cities.

An initial declaration was signed by key representatives of the corporate sector – CEOs of big companies and heads of business associations - in July 2005 in Bratislava at the international conference Twin City Industrial Platform (Industriellenvereinigung 2006: 2).

There is strong potential for regional cooperation to solve various problems arising under economic pressure such as environmental risks, noise and traffic and to improve the social structure of the region. This concept can well promote the supposed unique selling proposition (USP) under such headings as ‘highly qualified region’, ‘balanced region’, ‘open-minded region’ or ‘sustainable region’. The bipolarity of the region has the advantage of balancing peripheral areas and exploiting the socio-economic potentials of Vienna and Bratislava more efficiently.

However, the twin city scenario is still rather business-driven and lacks the necessary institutional background. Representatives of the corporate sector prepared this vision in order to promote their business activities and goals. Yet it is unclear who can take on responsibility for the marketing communication of the “twincity” Brand, and for implementing activities. Moreover it is an open question which role smaller municipalities in the hinterland of the capital cities can play.

4.3 CENTROPE

CENTROPE is the name of a regional cross-border cooperation initiative. It was launched in September 2003 when state and local governments in the border quadrangle of Austria, Czech Republic, Hungary and Slovakia signed a cooperation treaty in the Austrian town of Kittsee. They agreed to jointly establish and promote the Central European Region (Krajatis et al. 2003). Furthermore they stressed the aim of developing the CENTROPE region as a framework for increasing wealth and sustainable growth across the Central European area, which is living and working space for about 6 million people.

After the accession of Slovakia, Czech Republic and Hungary to the EU, this newly established joint region as a whole is part of the European internal market. The urban agglomeration axis Vienna-Bratislava is the intersection of major international transport routes and secures access to dominant centres in the entire EU.

The necessary institutional network has been established by means of an INTERREG III A project. Currently there is a formal cooperation structure, including an advisory board, a steering committee, working groups and a project secretariat. Cooperation materializes in high-profile annual conferences and pilot projects on issues such as biotechnology, labour market, regional management, sports and culture (Project Secretariat CENTROPE 2007).

Generally, the favourable strategic location, the high quality of the infrastructure and skilled labour forces were highlighted as the principal competitive advantages of the CENTROPE region. This region might serve as a bridgehead to growing markets in the new EU Member States and become one of the major beneficiaries of EU enlargement. (CENTROPE Consortium 2005: 3). As the CENTROPE region comprises the most prosperous regions of the four participating countries, it can draw on their top potentials.

On the other hand it should be mentioned that the entire CENTROPE initiative seems to be a scientific or political construction rather than a naturally shaped region. Some sophisticated strategic management and marketing activities such as a regional image analysis have been implemented. However, it seems that cooperation has been more successful in its external dimension – i.e., in terms of marketing and promotion, image making and maintenance – than in its internal dimension, including the population's identification with the cross-border region or transboundary policy-making and cooperation.

Such a concept relies on spontaneous identification and a sense of togetherness among stakeholders within the larger region. Many consider the region to be artificial, since in includes area functionally oriented towards other centres, like the Czech town of České Budějovice, or which have only weak ties with the centres of the CENTROPE region, like southern Hungary.

Imbalanced and heterogeneous socio-economic conditions in the participating countries, language barriers, examples of deficient behaviour as well as scepticism and prejudices might slow down or even compromise efforts to consolidate CENTROPE, which is a best practice case in terms of multilateral cross-border cooperation in Europe.

5 Conclusions

Increasing and accelerating competition among European regions will strongly influence urban development as well as regional policy. Each region strives to define and exploit a favourable position in this competition. As we have seen in the case of the metropolitan region Vienna-Bratislava, highly coordinated efforts and mutual cooperation across national boundaries is urgent and beneficial.

If they are to be successful in the long run, European regions have to mobilise all resources and to find the most efficient ways to cooperate at the international level. Voluntary cooperation, information exchanges, active representation, and marketing tools are considered crucial for successful positioning in competition between regions (Miosga 2005: 113).

Competition between regions and the tasks resulting from it are strong motivating factors. If a region manages to fully develop and display its inner potential, it will achieve a high quality of life.

Although the Vienna-Bratislava metropolitan region has already adopted a wide scope of strategic efforts such as CENTROPE and some rather business-driven marketing initiatives such as 'twincity', it still faces strategic challenges. The CENTROPE strategy seems to be better fitted for cooperation at the strategic level, but in terms of a comprehensive strategy for Vienna and Bratislava the twin city concept is thought to be a more specifically marketable with regard to competitiveness.

EU enlargement, accelerating competition between European regions, demographic shifts as well as pressure to develop innovative patterns in regional policy give strong impetus to both the Austrian and the Slovakian parts of the Vienna-Bratislava metropolitan region to achieve strategic, balanced, appropriate and sophisticated cross-border cooperation. If the region succeeds in managing the complex interactions between the two parts, it might become a model area for cross-border cooperation and a growth engine in Central Europe.

References

Centrope Consortium (2005) We grow together – together we grow. CENTROPE vision 2015. Available online: http://centrope.info/static/files/baerdtneu/We_grow_together_Together_we_grow.pdf, visited on 15.02.2007

Dettmar M (2001) Stadtmarketing [City marketing]. Available online: http://www.geo-zine.de/stama.htm, visited on 14.02.2007

Finka M (2005) Vienna – Bratislava Region. Between Cooperation and Competition. In: Giffinger R (ed) Competition between Cities in Central Europe: Opportunities and Risks of Cooperation, ROAD, Bratislava, 123–135

Finka M, Zigrai F (2005) Relationship among "Ideal European Regions" and "Real European Regions" on the Example of Border Region Bratislava – Vienna – Selected metascientific and applied aspects. Institute of Spatial Planning and Urban Design, Faculty of Architecture of the Slovak University of Technology, Bratislava

Giffinger R (ed) (2005) Competition between Cities in Central Europe: Opportunities and Risks of Cooperation. ROAD, Bratislava

Hall P (2006) 'Positioning Vienna-Bratislava': Which Future Development Strategy? Potentials of City Marketing and Cooperation in the Competition of the Cities. Unpublished

Hofmann T (2004) Vienna Today. Prestel, München, Berlin London New York

Hrdina V (ed), Hanus J, Slimák D, Tvrdoň J, Konček J, Rehák Š, Gregáčová J, Minarových P, Vargicová G (2002a) Joint chapter for the Vienna Bratislava Region Background Report. Aurex, Bratislava

Hrdina V (ed), Hanus J, Slimák D, Tvrdoň J, Konček J, Rehák Š, Gregáčová J, Minarových P, Vargicová G (2002b) Podkladová správa pre zhodnotenie regiónu Viedeň Bratislava [Vienna Bratislava Region Evaluation Background Report]. Aurex, Bratislava

Industriellenvereinigung (= Landesgruppen Wien, Niederösterreich und Burgenland der Österreichischen Industriellenvereinigung) (2006) Central European Region. Europa Region Mitte. Twin City Wien – Bratislava. Partly available online: http://www.iv-mitgliederservice.at/iv-all/publikationen/file_351.pdf, visited on 15.02.2007

Kotler P, Haider D, Rein I (1994) Standortmarketing. Wie Städte, Regionen und Länder gezielt Investitionen, Industrien und Tourismus anziehen [Place Marketing, How Cities, Regions and Lands attract Investments, Industry and Tourism]. Econ, Düsseldorf, Wien, New York, Moskau

Kozma G (2006) Place Marketing for Geographers and Geography Teachers, Kossuth Egyetemi Kiado. Debreceni Egyetem, Debrecen

Krajatis C, Neunteufl G, Steiner R (2003) Regional Analysis of the CENTROPE Region. DIANE Projekt. Österreichisches Institut für Raumplanung, Vienna

Magistrat der Stadt Wien (2004) Strategieplan Wien [Strategy plan for Vienna]. Available online: http://www.wien.gv.at/stadtentwicklung/strategieplan/, visited on 15.02.2007

Magistrat der Stadt Wien (2005) Stadtentwicklungsplan 2005 [Urban Development Plan]. Available online: http://www.wien.gv.at/stadtentwicklung/step/step06.htm, visited on 5.02.2007

Miosga M (2005) Munich´s city-cooperations between image-building and learning processes. In: Giffinger R (ed) Competition between Cities in Central Europe: Opportunities and Risks of Cooperation. ROAD, Bratislava, 108–122

Project Secretariat CENTROPE (2007) 'CENTROPE – Central European Region' (website). Available online: http://centrope.info/baernew, visited on 15.02.2007

Inter-urban cooperation in the German-Polish-Czech triangle

Robert Knippschild

Leibniz Institute of Ecological and Regional Development, Dresden

1 Cities in need of cross-border cooperation

This paper deals with inter-urban cooperation across national borders in the German-Polish-Czech triangle. In contrast to the other two contributions in this chapter, it focuses on cooperation on a smaller scale between neighboring cities (Görlitz/Zgorzelec) and in an urban-regional context (Zittau-Bogatynia-Hrádek nad Nisou).

It therefore begins by underlining the difficult starting position for cooperation in the German-Polish-Czech triangle and the simultaneous need for cooperation between cities, examining the challenges facing cooperation and the potential for cross-border solutions. Two processes in the evolution of inter-urban cooperation are then traced, considering the history, institutions, processes, results, and benefits of inter-urban cooperation, and identifying significant external factors influencing cross-border, inter-urban cooperation: administrative and political structures, as well as the legal framework, EU enlargement and transnational organizations. Finally the paper discusses the perspectives of inter-urban cooperation in drawing conclusions from the empirical findings.

The paper is based on two case studies of inter-urban cooperation:

- "Europe City Görlitz/Zgorzelec" on the German-Polish border
- "City Network Small Triangle Zittau-Bogatynia-Hrádek nad Nisou" in the immediate German-Polish-Czech border triangle (see fig. 1).

Both case studies have entailed an in-depth empirical examination of the benefits of transboundary cooperation for urban development in border regions and the main influencing factors. In both cases, twelve experts were interviewed about their experience with inter-urban cooperation (Knippschild forthcoming).

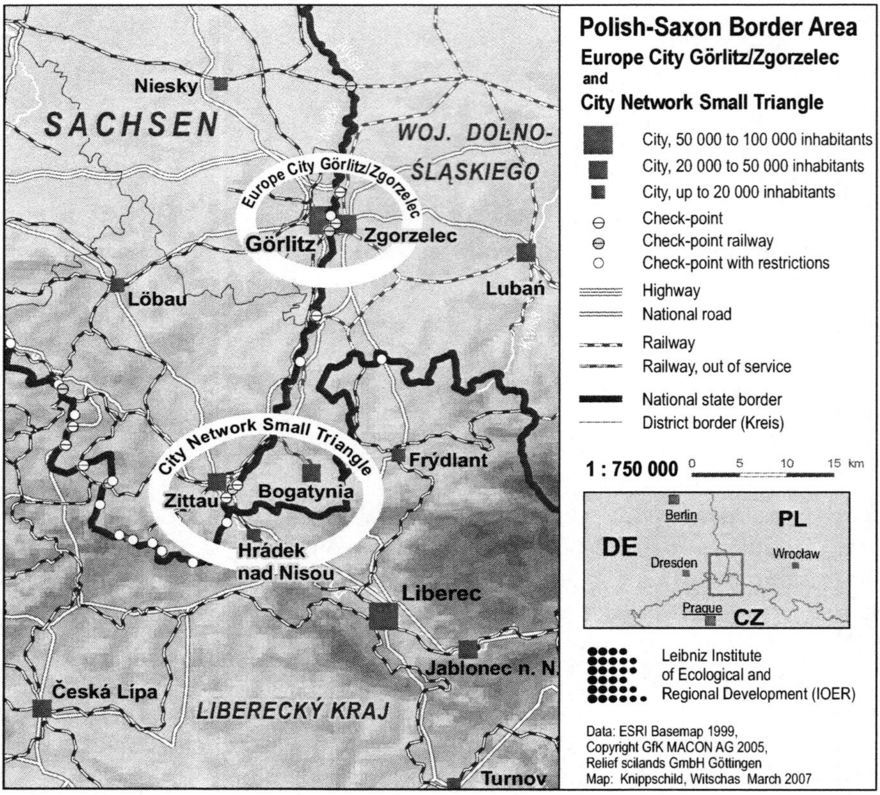

Figure 1. Location of the two case studies in the German-Polish-Czech border triangle

2 The starting position in the German-Polish-Czech triangle

2.1 Periphery cities in a weak region

The cities Görlitz and Zgorzelec are located directly on the border river Neiße/Nysa. The two cities form a single urban unit. Görlitz has about 58,000 inhabitants, Zgorzelec about 33,000. Zittau, Bogatynia and Hrádek nad Nisou are located in the border triangle between Germany, Poland and the Czech Republic at a distance of 5-10 km from each other. Zittau and Bogatynia each have around 25.000 inhabitants, Hrádek nad Nisou about 7,000 (Statistisches Landesamt des Freistaats Sachsens 2005: 26f., 45f.; Stadtverwaltung Zittau & Regioplan Ingenieure 2005: 27)

From the national perspective, the five cities under study are located peripherally. The German and Polish cities have suffered particularly strongly from the consequences of economic transition and demographic change. Görlitz and Zittau lost between 15 and 20 per cent of their population between 1991 and 2006. The Polish Zgorzelec has also been affected by demographic change, albeit to a lesser extent. The unemployment rate of over 25 per cent in Görlitz, Zgorzelec, Zittau and Bogatynia is higher than the regional and national average. Only Hrádek nad Nisou still benefits from population increase and low unemployment due to its proximity to the prospering regional centre of Liberec (Regioplan Ingenieure 2005: 27; Leibniz Institut für Länderkunde 2006: 28).

2.2 Different administrative structures and its implications

Inter-urban cooperation between these cities is hampered by differing administrative systems in Germany, Poland, and the Czech Republic. While German federalism has up to six administrative levels, the administrative systems in Poland and the Czech Republic are more centralized and have only four, respectively three administrative levels.

In a neighborhood conflicts may arise between two or more partners at any time. There are different mechanisms for coping with conflicts, like hierarchic control, compensation, or the centralization of decisions. Many are based on the threat of hierarchical problem-solving systems involving national public organizations that may solve the conflict, but not respect the partners' interests. They are therefore motivated to cope with conflicts through cooperative action, avoiding hierarchical control. Scharpf & Benz call this "cooperation in the shadow of hierarchy" or "negative coordination" (1991: 627; cf. also Frey 2003: 458f.).

The clash of different hierarchical systems along borders causes multi-level governance. National hierarchies do not operate in a transboundary context. Transboundary cooperation can thus not be said to proceed under a "shadow of hierarchy". The participating actors have to be cooperative although there is no threat of hierarchical sanctions. Asymmetrical administrative and hierarchical structures in public administration consequently hamper transboundary cooperation.

Besides different administrative systems the cooperating cities have to cope with different resources within administrations. In general, German municipalities have still more staff than the Polish or Czech local authorities (see tab. 1). For example, while a whole municipal department in Görlitz is in charge of urban development, a single city architect has to cope with almost the same task in the Zgorzelec municipality.

Table 1. Differing manpower in municipalities in the both cases (source: oral information, own calculation)

	Number of staff in municipalities*	Inhabitants per employee
Europe City Görlitz/Zgorzelec		
Görlitz	880	65
Zgorzelec	95	350
City Network Small Triangle		
Zittau	85	304
Bogatynia	120	213
Hrádek nad Nisou	27	271

* Concerns only the core administration without municipal enterprises and employment programs

2.3 Challenges of cooperation and scope for cross-border solutions

Since the enlargement of the European Union (EU) in May 2004, Poland and the Czech Republic have been full Member States. Nevertheless, cross-border cooperation still faces various challenges.

The borders in the German-Polish-Czech triangle can be described as "hard borders". The language barrier between German, Polish and Czech is significant, exacerbated by the low level of competence in Polish and

Czech among Germans. It is often hard to find professional translators and interpreters owing to the increasing demand for translating services (Leibenath & Knippschild 2005: 83).

The difficult history of Germany, Poland and the Czech Republic hampers cross-border cooperation. Tragic historical experience in World War II, flight and displacement still cause prejudices and reservations. Under these conditions, building trust between the cooperating actors remains a challenge (Klein-Hitpaß, Leibenath & Knippschild 2006: 60).

Due to the history of the three countries, experience with and a tradition of cross-border cooperation tends to be limited to the post-1990 period. Cities in western European borderlands have longer experience with cooperation, while cities in the German-Polish-Czech triangle have lagged behind. At the same time the pressure for cross-border cooperation has grown. EU directives and EU funds increasingly require and allow intensive cooperation in urban development in borderlands (Euregio Egrensis 2006: 4).

The need for cross-border and inter-urban cooperation arises from common problems and challenges in the cities under study. Almost all cities in the border triangle suffer from their peripheral location, high unemployment, shrinking population, and out migration, as well as deficiencies in the technical and social infrastructure.

Joint action and projects have therefore been proposed in the following fields:

- overcoming the peripheral location by enhancing accessibility and the transport infrastructure;
- enhancing attractiveness for investors by coordinated and joint location marketing;
- coordinated strategic urban development; joint land-use planning and land-use management; coordinated brown-field development;
- sharing of functions and social infrastructure;
- coordinated sectoral planning (e.g. technical infrastructure);
- coping with housing vacancies and shortages by supporting joint housing markets and
- safeguarding joint interests; joint lobbying of national and regional governments.

This list shows that cities in the German-Polish-Czech border triangle need to work together since there is broad latitude for cross-border solutions and a back log in cooperation. Nonetheless, the point of departure for transboundary, inter-urban cooperation is still difficult.

3 The evolution of inter-urban cooperation

This section focuses on two inter-urban cooperation processes. After going into the history of cooperation, the internal factors influencing inter-urban cooperation are examined, as well as the institutions of cooperation and the progress of communication processes. Finally, the results and benefits of cooperation are considered in detail.

3.1 History of cooperation

In both cases, the tradition of cooperation has been relatively short. Due to the "iron curtain", cross-border cooperation before 1990 was limited to nationally controlled activities. Personal contacts between Germans and Poles were impossible. After regime change in 1990, self-determined cross-border cooperation between municipalities began to develop. In 1991 the Euroregion Neiße-Nisa-Nysa was established as a cross-border association of municipalities and the first Euroregion on Germany's eastern borders. In the same year, a cooperation contract between the cities of Görlitz and Zgorzelec was signed. To begin with, cooperation tended to concentrate on cultural and social events (Association of European Border Regions 2000: B2 – 38, Jajeśniak-Quast & Stokłosa 2000: 77–88).

Some ten years later, cross-border cooperation in the German-Polish-Czech triangle reached a further stage. Görlitz and Zgorzelec proclaimed the "Europe City Görlitz/Zgorzelec" and committed themselves to joint urban development. In 2002 a two-year project intensified cooperation between the two cities. This project "City 2030 – Joint Vision for the Europe City Görlitz/Zgorzelec" was funded by the German Ministry for Education and Research and focused on developing strategies for joint urban development through an intensive communication process between the two municipalities. One year before a cross-border regional development concept was elaborated for Zittau, Bogatynia and Hrádek nad Nisou and the three cities signed an agreement establishing the City Network Small Triangle. The cross-border regional development concept was funded by the Community Initiative INTERREG II C. With these activities, the cities developed cooperation towards joint strategic urban development (Friedrich et al. 2005: 15f., Gowin 2003: 39).

Another important mile stone in the history of inter-urban cooperation in the German-Polish-Czech triangle was EU enlargement in May 2004. Official festivities were staged by the German, Polish and Czech governments in the presence of the heads of government Gerhard Schröder, Leszek Miller and Vladimír Špidla in the border triangle close to Zittau.

Finally in December 2007 the Schengen Treaty came into force in Poland and the Czech Republic with border controls ceasing to exist.

3.2 Institutions of cooperation and the communication process

Any kind of cooperation requires a minimum of institutional framework in order to provide some kind of security for the cooperating actors. Without any institutional or legal framework, cooperation risks failing (Scharpf 1997: 112, 135). Both case studies of inter-urban cooperation have transboundary cooperation institutions of cooperation available. These institutions involve organizational, political and financial structures in the cooperating municipalities that help structure and stabilize cooperation processes by providing the needed security.

For both cooperation processes, steering committees have been established. In Görlitz/Zgorzelec a steering committee consisting of the mayors and city council members operated throughout the project City 2030. This committee has not been maintained on a standing basis since completion of the project. Today a coordination committee is active – although not on the highest political level. In the City Network Small Triangle a standing steering committee is also in charge of preparing political decisions on cooperation between the three cities.

Since hierarchical control and sanctions do not exist in transboundary cooperation – owing to a lack of formal transboundary institutions – communication is the only possible by means of interaction in transboundary, inter-urban cooperation. Therefore the communication process between cooperating cities is of particular interest. Working groups were established for substantive exchanges in both case studies. The five working groups in Görlitz/Zgorzelec were intensified during the City 2030 project with regular and frequent meetings and workshops. Meanwhile, some working groups again meet only irregularly and rarely. The intensity of communication between Görlitz and Zgorzelec decreased after the project City 2030 ended while continuing on a high level in the City Network Small Triangle. Seven thematic and projects groups meet regularly, with between 20 and 30 meetings monthly. This high density of meetings guarantees continuity in communication between the participating actors.

For political decision-taking the cities under study established different political institutions. A joint city council meeting took place in Görlitz/Zgorzelec during the City 2030 project. Joint meetings are otherwise not regular. Decisions are prepared in the coordination committee but finally taken separately by the Görlitz and Zgorzelec city councils. In contrast, the City Network Small Triangle has institutionalized joint meetings of the three city councils. At least twice a year, the three city councils meet to take decisions and give strategic orientation to the city network.

Both case studies had temporary secretariats for coordinating inter-urban cooperation. A German-Polish secretariat was established within the City 2030 project in Görlitz. It was in charge of preparing and organizing workshops and seminars, translating and interpreting for the working groups as well as for public relations. Furthermore, the secretariat functioned as a contact point for citizens and initiatives in the two cities who were interested in the project. In the City Network Small Triangle an external consultant initiated, facilitated and coordinated cooperation from the outset. After four years, the three cities decided to take over coordination because funding ceased. Today three internal coordinators – one in each city – are in charge of organizing and managing the cooperation process. The initiative for internal coordination highlights the political will to institutionalize inter-urban cooperation in the City Network Small Triangle. However, the actors involved in transboundary cooperation miss the thematic input previously provided by external coordination.

Both cases benefited from temporary external funding. While cooperation between Görlitz and Zgorzelec declined after external funding within the City 2030 project ceased, the cities in the City Network Small Triangle established a joint budget for transboundary cooperation. Each of the three cities contributes one Euro per inhabitant per year into this fund. With this budget, some € 60.000 Euro is made available per year to fund cooperation. The cities thus commit themselves to long-term cooperation by contributing monetary resources. Once a year a joint budget plan is elaborated and finalized by a joint city council meeting. The joint fund highlights the importance of self-commitment by the participating municipalities to inter-urban and transboundary cooperation.

3.3 Results and benefit of cooperation

While the results of cooperation are obvious, the benefits for the cities are hard to measure. The benefits of inter-urban cooperation depend on political consequences. If the results of cooperation – like joint strategies – are not considered within everyday decisions on urban development, the benefits of cooperation remain symbolic. Since decisions and implementation in urban development are long-term proceedings, there is a time shift between the results of cooperation, like joint strategy, and the benefits, like coordinated transboundary urban development.

As far as the results of cooperation are concerned, both case examples have been fairly successful. Cooperation between Görlitz and Zgorzelec in the City 2030 project produced several elements of a joint vision of inter-urban cooperation. The cities agreed on a cooperation directive, on joint projects of strategic importance, and on cross-sectional priorities for cooperation. The main ideas have been the elaboration of a cross-sectional development strategy for both cities, a joint center for business development, and the intensive participation of citizens in the process of joint urban development. All these aspects were incorporated by modifying the agreement between the two cities at the end of the project. In case of the City Network Small Triangle, the main results of cooperation have so far been a regional development concept, which has already been up-dated into a joint development plan, and several strategic projects. The most important projects for inter-urban development are a transboundary network of business zones and the transboundary management of settlement area.

The main difference between both the two case examples is how the cooperating cities deal with the agreed results of cooperation. In the case of Görlitz and Zgorzelec, the agreed issues have had almost no consequences – although the agreements were incorporated into the cooperation agreement. At least the cross-sectional development strategy has since been implemented – but not as a joint project. The city of Zgorzelec initiated this strategy but was disappointed at the lack of engagement on the part of the Germans. The municipality of Görlitz regarded the strategy as a Polish project and collaborates passively rather than actively by issuing official comments. These reasons are misunderstandings, differences in administrative structures and working methods. A contact point for coordination and facilitation in such cases is still lacking.

The situation has been different in the case of the City Network Small Triangle: Agreements about strategies and projects have been followed by political consequences and implementation. The city councils are informed regularly about the progress of inter-urban cooperation and control implementation. Moreover, the three coordinators in the municipalities guarantee continuity in cooperation and mediate when problems or misunderstandings arise.

4 External influencing factors

Besides these internal factors, external factors can be identified that have influenced the success of transboundary inter-urban cooperation. The most important are asymmetrical administrative and political structures, as well as the legal framework for cooperation, EU enlargement, and transnational organizations.

4.1 Administrative and political structures

The two case studies have shown that different transformation paths, administrative and political structures have influenced inter-urban, transboundary cooperation between Germany, Poland and the Czech Republic.

In Poland and the Czech Republic, administrative and political structures are meanwhile well established and much more stable than some years ago. Nevertheless, personnel turnover in municipalities after political elections is still a problem, since the establishment of trust between cooperating actors is made difficult. Eastern Germany has a different problem. In most cases the West German administrative system was imposed in Eastern Germany, accompanied by a transfer of top personnel to accelerate the process of transformation. This still leads to uncertainties and frustration among East German municipal staff. These effects have been re-inforced by the constant threat of job losses due to the general need to reduce the public service in East Germany.

Differences in national administrative and political structures in the cooperating countries have a negative impact on transboundary cooperation. In particular, the Polish system is more centralistic with protracted decision making processes, while decentralized structures have been well established in Eastern Germany and the Czech Republic. In general, differences in competence and administrative structures still hinder transboundary cooperation. For instance, environmental protection proved to be a difficult field of cooperation in the border cities of Görlitz/Zgorzelec since responsible for environmental protection lies not with the municipality of Zgorzelec but with the district. However, the two case studies also showed that different administrative and political structures are often put forward as an excuse when problems arise in cooperative action for other – often internal – reasons within the municipalities.

Differences in the resources available to municipalities in Germany, Poland and the Czech Republic had a much greater impact. Small municipalities were by no means less capable of transboundary cooperation than bigger ones. German municipalities tend to have greater personnel resources but in the case examples appeared complex and inflexible to their Polish and Czech partners. Strong specialization, numerous departments and narrow professional staff profiles make cooperation difficult. Where a coordinator for transboundary coordination was lacking, Polish and Czech partners judged German municipalities to be complex and confusing. Municipalities in Poland and the Czech Republic are smaller but more flexible and more capable of transboundary cooperation. In the cooperation processes under study, smaller municipalities were better able to cope with unexpected circumstances, being more flexible and willing to improvise.

Furthermore, differences in the political systems and in relations between politics and administration in the cooperating countries affect transboundary cooperation. In Poland and the Czech Republic decision-making in municipalities is rather hierarchical. Mayors have a strong position in decision-making processes. They prepare strategic decisions, with the municipal council making the final decision, which is then implemented by the administration. Power in German municipalities is more fragmented between the council, the heads of department, and the mayor. In Görlitz/Zgorzelec, this led to stagnation in the implementation of transboundary projects and to confusion and frustration among the Polish partners.

In all cases, political legitimization influenced transboundary cooperation. Lacking political legitimization caused uncertainty among participating administrative actors and finally led to blockades in the implementation of transboundary projects. Administrative staff suffered from a lack of support for transboundary activities and feared negative consequences. Although these fears proved unjustified, they at least temporarily hindered the implementation of transboundary projects. The reasons are to be found in a lack of comprehension among political decision makers for cooperation processes. Blockades through lacking political legitimization could be avoided where political decision makers were informed about the cooperation process and participated in transboundary working groups and project groups. Furthermore, a political willingness for transboundary cooperation proved necessary.

Another – fortunately temporary – impact on transboundary cooperation had been exerted by the current political situation in Poland. The strong national-conservative orientation and Euro-scepticisms of the national government under the Prime Ministers Kazimierz Marcinkiewicz and Kaczyński in Poland had a negative influence on transboundary cooperation at the local and regional levels.

4.2 Legal framework, EU enlargement and transnational organizations

Analysis of the case studies shows that EU enlargement, the European legal framework, and transnational organizations have influences transboundary cooperation between Germany, Poland and the Czech Republic – but to differing extents.

A major obstacle to date has been the lack of a legal framework for cooperation. Agreements on transboundary cooperation between cities – for instance the agreement between Görlitz and Zgorzelec – have no standing in public international law. In fact, such agreements are more in the nature of declarations of intention and are not legally binding. Common transboundary projects and activities have been inhibited due to this absence of a legal framework. The establishment of transboundary institutions has also been difficult, almost illegal. A common budget for the cities Zittau, Bogatynia and Hrádek nad Nisou in the German-Polish-German Triangle is legally dubious and cannot provide a basis for investment. The more concrete transboundary cooperation becomes, the more of an obstacle the lack of a legal framework has proved.

High hopes were placed in EU Enlargement in May 2004, especially in Poland and the Czech Republic. Before enlargement, many obstacles to cooperation were reduced to the external EU border. In general, EU enlargement fell short of expectations, since many obstacles remained after the accession of Poland and the Czech Republic. Disappointment and resignation were apparent in the borderland. Despite faster border controls, transboundary cooperation was hardly facilitated. Different national interpretations of EU directives still hinder the harmonization of the legal framework in borderlands. Transboundary project funding has still been complicated in the funding period 2000–2006 by the structure of funding programmess and the tardy establishment of organizational structures for implementating EU funding in Poland and the Czech Republic.

However, the psychological impacts of EU enlargement should not be underestimated. Both case studies showed that before May 2004 there was a kind of euphoria and positive attitude to all kinds of transboundary cooperation. In certain cases, enlargement was even the motive for engaging in transboundary cooperation. Furthermore, greater self-confidence was apparent, particularly in Polish and Czech local government and administration. However, reservations and resignation have meanwhile spread owing, for instance, to restrictions on labor mobility. Polish and Czech sometimes feel like "second class European citizens".

Transnational organizations had limited influence on transboundary co-operation in the cases under study. The greatest influence was attributed to the EU for their funding programmes. All the cooperation projects examined would not have been possible without the help of at least occasional European funding. Interestingly, the Euroregions had little or even negative influence on transboundary cooperation, although they constitute the only transboundary institutions on the local level. The Euroregions hardly supported transboundary cooperation in the three case examples. To some extent they even hindered transboundary activities. This was firstly due to the inappropriate organizational structure of the Euroregions with separate secretaries in each country and limited resources and competences, and secondly because the Euroregions feared competition in transboundary activities.

5 Prospects for inter-urban cooperation: Continuity and coordination

Since the external factors discussed cannot be changed, they have to be accepted and coped with. This paper has shown that, leaving external factors aside, there are many opportunities for designing and managing inter-urban cooperation to influence its success.

The case studies show that continuity is one of the most important aspect when designing and managing transboundary cooperation in urban development. Transboundary cooperation in general is complicated and lengthy. It will therefore succeed only if it offers a long-term perspective. Building trust, exchanging information in a multi-lingual context, and reaching agreement on joint priorities takes a long time. Furthermore, the participating actors need a long-term perspective for cooperation if they are to be motivated, since no hierarchical sanctions come into play ("shadow of the future" instead of "shadow of hierarchy").

Continuity can be promoted by ensuring a steady process of communication and providing suitable discussion forums. Agreements concluded in inter-urban cooperation should be taken into accounting in political decisions on urban development. Appropriate political decisions are also required to ensure the implementation of joint projects.

The second important aspect when designing and managing inter-urban cooperation is to provide coordination. Contact points or secretariats can facilitate communication and again promote continuity. These offices should be staffed equally by representatives from all cooperating municipalities. The coordinators should have experience in administrative and enough autonomy to avoid hierarchical control and chains of command.

The cooperating municipalities should provide coordinators with all the necessary information and access to all levels of the hierarchy.

This paper has stressed that inter-urban cooperation is by no means an easy field of action, and one that requires careful preparation and management. Inter-urban cooperation that is both continuous and well coordinated can contribute to the sustainable development of cities in borderlands by identifying and implementing joint solutions, strategies and projects.

References

Association of European Border Regions (2000) Practical Guide to Cross-border Cooperation. Gronau. Available online: http://www.aebr.net/publikationen/pdfs/lace_guide.en.pdf, visited on 20.09.2007.

Euregio Egrensis Arbeitsgemeinschaft Bayern e.V. (2006) Euregio News letter 01/2006. Available online : http://www.euregio-egrensis.de/presse/newsletter2006_01.pdf, visited on 04.09.2006

Frey R (2003) Regional Governance zur Selbststeuerung territorialer Subsysteme [Regional Governance for Self-Government of Territorial Subsystems]. In: Informationen zur Raumentwicklung 8/9.2003, 451–462

Friedrich K, Knippschild R, Kunert M, Neumann I (2005) Auf dem Weg zu einem gemeinsamen Leitbild für die Europastadt Görlitz/Zgorzelec [On the Path Towards a Joint Vision for the Europe City Görlitz/Zgorzelec]. In: Friedrich K, Knippschild R, Kunert M, Meyer-Künzel M, Neumann I(eds) Zwei Grenzstädte wachsen zusammen – Im Zukunftsdialog zur Europastadt Görlitz/Zgorzelec [Two border Cities Grow Together – A Discussion About the Future towards the Europe City Görlitz/Zgorzelec]. Oekom, München, 13–20

Gowin M (2003) Trójkąt Trzech Krajów Zittau-Bogatynia-Hrádek - Das Dreiländereck Zittau-Bogatynia-Hrádek [The Border Triangle Zittau-Bogatynia-Hrádek]. In: Regionaler Planungsverband Oberlausitz-Niederschlesien / Wojewódzkie Biuro Urbanistyczne we Wrocławiu: Zusammenarbeit von Städten im Sächsisch-niederschlesischen Grenzraum [Inter-urban Cooperation in the Saxonian-Lower Silesian Borderland]. Bulletin des niederschlesisch-sächsischen Grenzgebietes Nr. 2/2003, 35–45

Jajeśniak D, Stokłosa K (2000) Geteilte Städte an Oder und Neiße. Frankfurt (Oder) – Słubice, Guben – Gubin und Görlitz – Zgorzelec 1945–1995 [Seperated Cities on Oder and Neiße River. Frankfurt (Oder) – Słubice, Guben – Gubin and Görlitz – Zgorzelec 1945–1995]. Frankfurter Studien zur Grenzregion Band 5. Berlin Verlag, Berlin

Klein-Hitpaß K, Leibenath M, Knippschild R (2006) Vertrauen in grenzüberschreitenden Akteursnetzwerken. Erkenntnisse aus dem deutsch-polnisch-tschechischen Kooperationsprojekt ENLARGE-NET [The Role of

Trust in Cross-border Networks of Actors. Findings from the German-Polish-Czech Cooperation Project ENLARGE-NET]. In: DISP 164 1/2006, 59–70

Knippschild R (forthcoming) Mit grenzüberschreitender Kooperation zu Territorialer Kohäsion? Gestaltung und Management von Kooperationsprozessen in der Raumentwicklung im deutsch-polnisch-tschechischen Grenzraum [With Cross-border Cooperation towards Territorial Cohesion. Designing and Managing Cooperation Processes in Spatial Development in the German-Polish-Czech Borderland]. IÖR, Dresden

Leibenath M, Knippschild R (2005) Systemic Evaluation of Cross-border Networks of Actors: Experience with a German-Polish-Czech Cooperation Project. In: Journal for Borderland Studies 20, 73–90

Leibniz-Institut für Länderkunde (ed) (2006) Konkretisierung der Leitbilder für den erweiterten deutsch-polnischen Grenzraum [Concretion of the Vision fort the Larger German-Polish Borderland]. Unpublished report, Leipzig

Scharpf F W (1997) Games Real Actors Play. Actor-Centred Institutionalism in Policy Research. Westview Press, Colorado, Oxford

Scharpf F W, Benz A (1991) Kooperation als Alternative zur Neugliederung? Zusammenarbeit zwischen den norddeutschen Ländern [Cooperation as an Alternative to Restructuring? Cooperation between the North-German Länder]. In: Schriften zur Innenpolitik und zur kommunalen Wissenschaft und Praxis. Nomos, Baden-Baden

Stadtverwaltung Zittau, Regioplan Ingenieure GmbH (2005) Zittau – Bogatynia – Hrádek nad Nisou. Städteverbund Kleines Dreieck. Gemeinsamer Entwicklungsplan. Endbericht. [Zittau – Bogatynia – Hrádek nad Nisou. City Network Small Triangle. Joint Development Plan. Final Report]. Zittau, Mannheim

Statistisches Landesamt des Freistaates Sachsen (ed) (2005) Statistisches Jahrbuch der Euroregion Neisse-Nisa-Nysa [Statistical Yearbook of the Euroregion Neisse-Nisa-Nysa]. Kamenz, Wrocław, Liberec

Functional complementarity as basis for inter-metropolitan collaboration and networking
A case study on cultural activities in Berlin and Warsaw

Ewa Korcelli-Olejniczak

Institute of Geography and Spatial Organization,
Polish Academy of Sciences, Warsaw

1 Transnational collaboration and networking

One of the features of contemporary transboundary cooperation is the development of a new spatial form that organizes relations between cities and regions - horizontal collaboration, which constitutes the basis for networking, defined as the establishment of "intertwined chains of social, political and economic relations" (Domański & Marciniak 2003: 5). Whereas transnational co-operation between cities is often a multi-layer phenomenon, it is frequently described as an example of the emergence of networks linking various institutions and activities functioning in urban areas (cf. e.g., FLD 2002).

Transnational urban co-operation is distinct from most other forms of networking in that

- it is usually based on a long-term perspective and
- there is a common goal which binds the members of a network (Minichbauer & Mitterdorfer 2000: 4).

Network cooperation between institutions and organizations serves as a tool for solving economic and social problems, including questions of ecological sustainability and long-term development. Networking between cities, based, for example, on similarities of functional structure, although a non-hierarchical tie, can support the promotion of the cities in hierarchical settlement systems. This can be explained on the basis of the concept of the innovative city (Domański 2000: 21), which is based on earlier theoretical assumptions about urban development (central places and urban systems), as well as on other concepts, such as self-organization theory and Prigogine's theory of dissipative structures. According to this concept, a system changes as a result of mutual interaction between its elements. This leads to the emergence of a new structure. The new order is characterized by new properties and can perform more advanced or more specialized functions. This means that "cities which expand as a result of changes in their macrostructure can move up in the hierarchy of the settlement system", and consequently "their functions grow in scope". It also implies that the scope and range of metropolitan functions can expand more effectively as a result of city networking.

City networking refers to inter-urban cooperation between public and private organizations in issues like services, innovation, training, and communication with the overall aim of achieving synergistic advantages (Schulman & Kaaninen 2002). City networking or – more generally – inter-urban cooperation and partnership can include more specific objectives such as strategic development, project orientation and mutual advocacy. The prospective achievements may be categorized into

- formation of a strategic framework,
- project implementation,
- capacity building,
- knowledge transfer, as well as
- place marketing and promotion (Nordregio 2004: 190–191).

These objectives and achievement categories can be applied to the analysis of inter-urban cooperation in the sphere of higher-order public services. Examples of best practices in this area include joint strategies of the Copenhagen-Malmö agglomeration in the field of education and the collaboration between Edinburgh and Glasgow in redeveloping canals and promoting cultural events (Nordregio 2004: 203).

After 1989, the web of European inter-urban linkages has been complemented by cities of Central and Eastern Europe, although their participation in European-wide networks is still dependent on socio-economic conditions in the individual countries and their position in European intergovernmental and other structures. Despite their economic growth and rigid transition, even the major cities of CEE are 'latecomers' with reference to the state of development of their metropolitan functions (Korcelli-Olejniczak 2004). In this respect the globalization level and their position in the European and global urban system broadly correspond with the character of their participation in the non-hierarchical inter-urban web. Only a small percentage of European-wide networks have been founded or based in Central and Eastern Europe (cf. Groth 2001). The situation is somewhat different with respect to regional networks. The Baltic Sea Region, for instance, is an exemplary case of intense and intricate networking and co-operation, based on common fields of action and common interests. One example is the Union of Baltic Cities (UBC), which was established in 1991 to promote sustainable development in the Baltic Sea Region. Various urban network development projects have been carried out in the framework of INTERREG II C, e.g., "The Baltic Palette", "Waterfront Urban Development" and "Baltic Rim Network". The recently completed project "Urban System and Urban Networking (USUN) in the Baltic Sea Region" focused – among others – on the international role of its major cities.

The functional complementarities of cities that are partners in the network is both an aim of and precondition for effective urban networking (Schulman & Kaaninen 2002). The phenomenon can be interpreted here as a specialization of each of the respective cities in activities that belong to the same sector of the economy but which are also mutually interdependent. In the case of industrial systems such interdependence typically occurs at the level of individual components or production phases (rather than complete assembled products) and is based upon *competitive advantages* of the partners (products) involved (Cornett & Snickars 2002). With regard to tertiary and quaternary sector functions, including cultural activities, functional complementarity involves specialization in products (projects) for which demand tends to increase more than proportionally once they are offered in the form of packages. Hence, functional complementarity is interpreted as a kind of functional specialization of cities conducive to the development of inter-city cooperation and city networking (cf. Aalbu 2004).

While cooperation between cities does not exclude competition between them, in the case of functional complementarity such competition may improve quality and enhance the overall development potential of cities performing specialized functions.

In fact, functional complementarity merely provides the capacity for inter-municipal cooperation and partnership. To be effectively utilized and to bring synergy effects in terms of increasing the competitiveness of individual cities within a larger urban system, it requires action on the part of local (sometimes regional and national) government. The involvement of urban administration in international, cross-boundary collaboration implies its capability to increase and organize such cooperation (Schulman & Kaaninen 2002). In fact, in the case of large cities (national capitals, in particular), this constitutes no real barrier to the development of partnership relations. Both the direction and profile of urban networking are likely to be influenced by the interplay of various political interests.

In the light of these considerations, this paper focuses on potential collaboration between two major cities of the Baltic Sea Region – Berlin and Warsaw – in the cultural sphere. It builds partly upon the concept of the Berlin-Warsaw trajectory formulated by A. Kukliński in the late 1990s (Domański 1999)[12].

Collaboration could be a tool for reconciling the needs and interests of the two capitals in functioning as major gateway cities between Western and Eastern Europe. The paper seeks potential for inter-urban cooperation and networking in the cultural field, perceiving this issue as an aspect of transboundary development problems. The contents analysis presented in section 3, embraces three strategic policy documents and two comprehensive cultural programmes to be carried out in Warsaw and Berlin in the coming years. Considering the different character of the two projects, the author does not suggest developing collaboration within these tasks, but rather – following the idea of networks – building a general cooperation programme based on functional complementarity.

2 Field of action: Culture

A city is directly positioned in the global urban hierarchy by economic metropolitan functions it performs and the degree to which they are developed. By contrast, non-economic metropolitan activities are often treated as an additional asset, which enhance the attractiveness of a city and make it 'more appealing' for investment capital. Recently, however, cultural functions have tended to be referred to as the activities that establish the overall potential of the city, hence constituting a value in its own right. The reciprocity of culture and other metropolitan functions is demonstrated by many conspicuous examples, such as Paris, London, New York, but also by relatively smaller cities like Vienna (cf. e.g., Lichtenberger 2000).

Investment in the cultural development of a city is usually profitable, though these activities are generally not ruled by short-term profit considerations. Also, they can expand as a consequence of inter-urban functional complementarity and collaboration. City networking in the sphere of

[12] This prospective development axis has been also referred to in more recent studies. For example, one of the future spatial development scenarios for Europe, generated in the framework of ESPON 3.2 project presents the emergence of a major concentration of urban and economic development within the area extending between Berlin, Prague, Budapest and Warsaw (IGEAT 2006)

cultural activities can contribute to the sustainable development of the individual partners.

In Poland, as in most other countries of Central and Eastern Europe, cultural networking is still in its early stages, due, among others, to the inconsistency of the legal framework and to numerous administrative barriers (cf. Minichbauer & Mitterdorfer 2000: 40).

2.1 Cultural heritage as a development asset

The 1992 European Treaty of Maastricht emphasizes the importance of cooperation between Member States and enables the Community to support and supplement their action in such areas as "improvement of the knowledge and dissemination of culture and history of the European peoples", "conservation and safeguarding of cultural heritage of European significance" and "non-commercial cultural exchange" (Maastricht Treaty 1992). Hence, the European Commission has established several programmes to support culture and to develop interrelations between countries and cities, such as 'Kaleidoskop' (1996–1999), 'Raphael' (1997–1999) and 'CONNECT' (2000) or – more recently – the new 'Culture Programme' (2007–2013).

Cultural heritage has also become one of the main policy aims put forward in the European Spatial Development Perspective (EU-COM 1999). This document points to the importance of spreading "cultural life throughout the EU, in particular by supporting the development of cultural facilities, upgrading public spaces and reviving commemorative sites". Cultural development is perceived as one of the components of regional development that "play a role of social and spatial balances" (EU-COM 1999: 30). The document stresses the importance of natural and cultural heritage as major factors of regional and urban development. The revival of cultural heritage has also been considered a major goal in the strategies for the sustainable development of metropolitan regions, as formulated in the framework of the URBAN 21 project (European Metropolitan Regions Project 1999).

In the course of European integration, the idea of co-operation and networking for the sake of economic, social and ecological sustainability has also involved Central and Eastern Europe (cf. Schulman & Kaaninen 2002). Culture has become one of the main fields of project-oriented co-operation between cities, as well as city-partnership relations.

2.2 Cultural functions as factors of metropolitan development in Berlin and Warsaw

Recent studies on the future role and position of Warsaw and Berlin perceive culture as an important component of the cities' development potential, and a considerable development factor (Korcelli-Olejniczak 2004; Kujath 2005). With respect to Warsaw, most authors stress the importance of increasing the attractiveness and the particular character of Poland's capital. Culture is one of them, next to knowledge-related and political functions. Thus, Jałowiecki (2004) points to a "unique cultural tender" as one of the characteristics that make the city recognizable among other urban centres. This is so, even though the author fails to observe a trend towards cultural promotion in Warsaw after 1990, as most cultural ventures of international importance, such as the Jazz Jamboree, the Warsaw Autumn festival, or the Chopin Festival, are actually older than the economic transformation of the country.

Similarly, Grochowski (2005: 243), when analyzing the level of international connectivity (position in the global network) of the Warsaw Metropolitan Area, qualifies cultural links as among the most important, constituting a basis for economic contacts. Warsaw and its immediate surroundings have notable cultural relations with other European countries, most intensely with Germany.

However, Grochowski (2005) stresses that most of the cultural ventures organized are single events and the contribution of foreign participants is mostly limited to organizational tasks. The two institutions that co-operate most actively on an international scale are the National Opera and the National Philharmonic Hall. The cultural position of Warsaw is usually described as strong on the national scale. The capital city is perceived as the number one cultural centre in Poland, in particular with respect to cultural institutions (Dembowska & Miazga 1996: 25) and as an intermediate centre as far as the European dimension is concerned (Kukliński 2000: 247).

A recent comparative study of Warsaw's and Berlin's metropolitan functions by the present author (Korcelli-Olejniczak 2004) points to the strong cultural position of Warsaw in the national dimension and quite optimistically evaluates the prospects of the city for attaining transnational importance in the field of culture by 2015. In semi-structured, in-depth interviews conducted by the author, 11 out of 15 experts expressed the opinion that the range or influence of Warsaw's cultural activities would become at least European-wide in the next decade. Furthermore, among the ten most important factors the study identified as contributing to the development of Warsaw's metropolitan functions, as many as eight were non-economic in nature, including the cultural function. In particular,

Warsaw's cultural functions were perceived as a major component of its function as a gateway city oriented towards the countries of Eastern Europe which are not yet members of the European Union.

The strong position of Berlin with respect to cultural functions has never been questioned. Opinions differ only insofar as the range of this activity is concerned. Putting aside the discussion about the enormous financial burden that the numerous well-established cultural institutions of both East and West Berlin have placed on the state and the federal budgets, the promotion of Berlin's role as the cultural metropolis of Germany is one of the major tasks of Berlin's state government, the Senate. In the comparative study referred to above (Korcelli-Olejniczak 2004), Berlin was ascribed an either European or global cultural position for the near future. The experts also identified the strong cultural function of Berlin as the most important factor supporting development of the city's other metropolitan functions.

Similarly, in analyzing the functional structure of Berlin, a number of authors stress the status of cultural activities as a major component of the city's development potential. Next to modern economic clusters in such fields as transportation technologies, medical and biological technologies, and software development, culture-oriented structures constitute the core sector of development in Berlin. Each month Berlin's tourist and cultural events attract several hundreds of thousands of visitors from all over the world (Kujath 2005: 130). Berlin also has a strong position among the global centres of culture and media producers, as in the German urban system the city is a privileged node in most organizational networks within the global media industry (Kraetke 2004: 2).

As employment statistics show (Korcelli-Olejniczak 2004), employment in Berlin during the 1990s and early 2000s in sectors covered by sections O and P of the Standard Industrial Classifications Index (SIC), namely recreation, sports, culture, community, social and personal service activities, grew by about one and a half percent annually. A similar growth of 1.56 percent was recorded in section H (hotels and restaurants).

With respect to Warsaw, a rather negative trend was observed in sections O and P between 1996 and 1999. 2000 marked the beginning of a slight but constant growth trend. Conversely, employment in section H in Warsaw has stagnated since 1990.

The employment data can only support the assumption that the development of the culture-related functions in Berlin is proceeding well, while in the case of Warsaw the potential is present though less successfully utilized.

3 Transnational range of cultural activities according to Berlin's and Warsaw's strategic planning documents

3.1 The Warsaw Strategy 2020

The new Warsaw Strategy 2020 (ZMSW 2005), a document elaborated by the city executive board and approved by the city council, includes a SWOT analysis, a mission, a vision and five strategic goals for the city's development until 2020.

With regard to goals, the number and diversity of museums, cultural parks, and historic monuments are to be increased and the facilities renovated in order to raise the attractiveness of Warsaw as a tourist centre. The conjunction of cultural and natural assets such as the Vistula River valley is a special feature of Warsaw, offering a unique climate and atmosphere. The document presents programmes for enhancing the natural conditions, landscape value and recreational character of these areas, making them attractive for both residents and tourists.

The Royal Road programme is a complex planning and cultural undertaking addressing the historically and culturally most valuable part of Warsaw extending from the old town to the King's summer residence in Wilanów.

In sum, the main assets of Warsaw as a capital of culture – according to the Warsaw Strategy – are its tradition, the combination of natural and cultural resources, the high quality of venues, especially music festivals, notably in the fields of classical music and jazz.

The gateway aspect of East-West relations and the unique role of culture in informing, mediating and uniting are not focal points of the Warsaw document. Nevertheless, these issues should be of key importance, especially when considering the functional complementarities between the large cities of the Baltic Sea Region and the cities of southern Central Europe like Prague, Budapest, and Vienna.

3.2 The 'BerlinStudie' and the Urban Development Concept

In the case of Berlin, development has been guided by a strategic document called 'BerlinStudie' (Der Regierende Bürgermeister von Berlin / Senatskanzlei 2001) and by the Urban Development Concept (SfS 2004). The latter document follows the basic philosophy of the BerlinStudie, especially identifying the role of certain metropolitan activities, mainly science-related functions and culture. The concept reports on activities in particular spatial planning fields in the city, and presents an analysis of assumptions about the spatial, as well as the economic and social development of Berlin. The field of cultural activities is a crucial issue in both documents.

The BerlinStudie identifies two main resources of the city: knowledge and East-West mediation. Berlin is presented as a city that offers special qualities as a centre of science and the knowledge-based economy, as well as a place where East meets West, a modern international gate-way city on the borders of Eastern and Western Europe. According to the document, Berlin's cultural sector is one of the city's main assets: the city is both a modern centre of artistic innovation and performance and a traditional venue of classical culture and the arts.

The BerlinStudie thoroughly investigates interdependencies between the above activities and stresses the importance of using cultural qualities as a basis for Berlin's position in the East-West relations. The city should take advantage of its cultural capacity to develop networking and trans-border co-operation between its cultural institutions and corresponding institutions in other major cities of Central and Eastern Europe. The study stresses the importance of concentrating on economic and cultural co-operation and reinforcing cultural interaction with Central and Eastern European regions between the Baltic and Black Seas.

The Urban Development Concept refers to culture as one of seven main aspects of urban development in Berlin. Cultural activities are perceived here as those that support tourism. Since 1990, Berlin's cultural qualities have gained the city third place among European metropolises as a tourist destination. In 2002, 4.75 million people visited the German capital. Apart from Berlin's theatres, opera houses, and museums, the city's main cultural assets include numerous avantgarde artistic events. The main attraction of Berlin as a tourist destination lies in the diversity of cultural events and institutions. In the framework of tourism and culture, the Urban Development Concept points to various tasks to be undertaken in supporting the rich cultural offerings of the city. The promotion of culture and tourism should include concrete events and institutions, cultural projects, congresses and trade fairs, as well as planning schemes for parts of the city of particular interest to tourists.

4 The "Royal Road" and the "Cultural Forum" as examples of cultural development planning programmes

One way to promote culture and tourism in urban development is offered by programmes for reorganizing and improving selected parts of the city which are of special interest to tourists. Such programmes may address traditional, old districts and areas of special historical and cultural value, or newer parts of the city, where tradition interacts with modernity. Many large cities (London, Rotterdam, Vienna) have established *cultural forums*, mosaics of cultural institutions, such as museums and libraries, together with commercial establishments – galleries, shops and coffee shops. These areas are mainly situated centrally in the city and, due to the complexity of their functions and character, constitute a special attraction for both residents and tourists. In Vienna there is the so called MuseumsQuartier (since: June 2001), located near the Hofburg, which unites various forms of the arts: from traditional culture (Leopold-Museum, Museum of Modern Art, etc) to modern off-culture facilities. Also, from the architectural perspective, the area constitutes a mixture of classic and modern, contemporary styles and directions.

Such an area of cultural diversity is being planned and developed in Berlin, whereas in the case of Warsaw, the programme Royal Road has been prepared to reinforce the historically most valuable parts of the city. Both programmes, although different in character, follow the aim of preserving the special cultural heritage of the cities, their style and uniqueness.

4.1 The Kulturforum in Berlin

The Kulturforum is a part of the Tiergarten District, since 1828 known as the Friedrichvorstadt. The elegant suburban villas of the 19th century were eventually substituted by noble buildings constructed by many well-known architects: Martin Gropius, Karl Gotthardt Langhans, Johann Heinrich Strack. After 1937, the Tiergarten District lost its character due to the Nazi planning by Albert Speer. The area was cut in two parts by the extremely wide North-South axis and developed into a representative embassy district. Most of the buildings were destroyed during the war. In the 1960s the Kulturforum became a separate area within the Tiergarten District, when decisions about the location of museums (Galerie des 20. Jahrhunderts – Neue Nationalgalerie; Gemäldegalerie) in the vicinity of the Philharmonic Hall were taken. The Philharmonic Hall (1960–63) and the State Library

(1967–78) were designed by the expressionist architect Prof. Hans Scharoun. The planning of the buildings in the Kulturforum along the Berlin wall was symbolic: the location of the cultural centre of West Berlin near the border was to be understood as a sign of the unity of the divided city. It was not until 1989 that the city fabric around the Kulturforum started to grow together. Only the central structure of the Forum still lacks a final form. In 2002, the Berlin Senate Department of Urban Development began to discuss the concept for extending and developing the Kulturforum. The programme Kultur-Forum involves planning and cultural policies. The important cultural facilities in the area and the outstanding architecture of the buildings are to be complemented by a high-quality open public space. This requires structural enlargements and garden-architectural arrangements. Apart from the cultural use of the area, the Kulturforum will have other functions, especially important for tourists, such as galleries, shops, restaurants and coffee shops.

The Kulturforum programme addresses an area of particular significance, both as far as the history and the future of Berlin are concerned. In completing the Kulturforum, the city will gain a place that will enhance the cultural and geopolitical uniqueness of Berlin.

4.2 The Royal Road in Warsaw

One of the goals of the National Strategy of Cultural Development for the years 2004–2013 is to create new tourist products (city & culture) in Poland's major cities: Warsaw, Cracow, Poznań, Gdańsk and Wrocław. The strategic programme "The Royal Road in Warsaw" was the first project initiated by the minister of culture in 2003.

The Royal Road is an area situated in the centre of the city, a route leading from the old town (with the royal castle), along Krakowskie Przedmieście and Nowy Swiat streets, Plac Trzech Krzyzy (Three Crosses Square) Aleje Ujazdowskie with the Ujazdowski and Lazienki parks, to the park-palace complex of Wilanów. It is historically and culturally the most valuable part of Warsaw, the longest route of its kind in Poland, with buildings, monuments and parks of significant architectonic value, a symbol of freedom, cultural diversity and tradition reaching back to the 16th century. The cultural institutions, monuments and urban space along the Royal Road have cultural and tourist potential of the greatest value and highest European standard. However, due to the poor condition of the infrastructure and the lack of promotion, Warsaw cannot use the potential of this area as a factor in metropolitan competitiveness. Therefore, the Royal Road strategy aims to preserve the cultural heritage and enhance national identity, as well as raising the attractiveness of Warsaw and its competitiveness on the European cultural tourism market.

Strategic activities include the utilization of public and urban assets, the preservation and promotion of resources of cultural institutions, the establishment of a management system, and cooperation with external partners, financing, etc. The route along the Royal Road is to become a multifunctional attraction for residents and visitors, a place where Poland is more visible in Europe.

5 Conclusions

Berlin and Warsaw – the two important nodes of the Baltic Sea Region straddling the borders of Eastern and Western Europe are usually perceived as competitors in the struggle for metropolitan functions. In this rivalry, Warsaw's position is rather subdominant, due both to Berlin's stronger embedment in the West and the power of the German economy. Nevertheless, Warsaw is succeeding in securing a niche of its own, and is not threatened by Berlin's dominance, especially owing to its strong, indeed unrivalled position in the Polish settlement system.

The concept of the Berlin-Warsaw trajectory (Domański 1999) anticipates the development of rather equivalent relations between the two cities, which would support the reinforcement of the position of individual regions situated along the European West-East axis. According to this approach – which is more seldom applied in regional studies than the competitive vision – relations between the two nodes of the trajectory, their functional interdependence, should be based on exchanges, cooperation, in fact on long-term partnership.

The function of culture is one such activity that can effectively provide a basis for inter-urban, and in this case transboundary, cooperation. In the field of culture, Berlin and Warsaw have original and unique assets at their disposal, which seem to be mutually complementary. This is comprehensively illustrated by the two cultural projects planned and realized in the cities. Taken together, the original cultural value of Berlin and Warsaw may counterbalance the potential of the three cultural metropolises of South-Central Europe, Prague, Budapest and Vienna.

Networking between cultural institutions, information and artistic exchanges may be an effective form of city promotion. Combined projects based on urban functional complementarity can contribute to a further expansion of cultural activities. They can also generate inter-city tourism, where selected cities represent single nodes in a tourist product network.

This form of cooperation supports the gateway functions of the large cities, making them recognizable as individuals, while intensifying the features that make them geopolitically distinguishable as a spatial cluster.

References

Aalbu H (2004) Potential for Polycentric Development in Europe. Nordic Centre for Spatial Development, Stockholm

Cornett A, Snickars F (2002) Trade and Foreign Direct Investments as Measures of Spatial Integration in the Baltic Sea Region. Geographia Polonica 75: 33–56

Dembowska Z, Miazga M (1996) Warszawa w strukturze osadniczej Polski [Warsaw in the Polish settlement system]. Instytut Gospodarki Przestrzennej i Komunalnej, Warsaw

Der Regierende Bürgermeister von Berlin / Senatskanzlei (2001) Die BerlinStudie. Strategien für die Stadt [The Berlin Study. Strategies for the city]. Regioverlag, Berlin

Domański R, Marciniak A (2003) Sieciowe koncepcje gospodarki miast i regionów [Network Concepts in the Urban and Regional Economy]. Polska Akademia Nauk, Komitet Przestrzennego Zagospodarowania Kraju, Warsaw

Domański R (2000) Miasto Innowacyjne [The Innovative City]. Polska Akademia Nauk, Komitet Przestrzennego Zagospodarowania Kraju, Warsaw

Domański R (ed) (1999) The Changing Map of Europe. The Trajectory Berlin-Poznań-Warsaw. Friedrich Ebert Stiftung, Warsaw

EU-COM (= European Commission) (1999) ESDP. European Spatial Development Perspective. Towards Balanced and Sustainable Development of the Territory of the European Union. Available online: http://europa.eu.int/comm/regional_policy/sources/docoffic/official/reports/pdf/sum_en.pdf, visited on 10.04.2006

European Metropolitan Regions Project (1999) Strategies for Sustainable Development of European Metropolitan Regions. Evaluation Report. Projektbüro 'Europäische Metropolregionen', Essen

FLD (= Forest and Landscape Denmark) (2002) Medium Sized Cities in Dialogue Around the Baltic Sea. Interreg IIIB/BSR Project. Info Nr 1. Forest and Landscape Denmark, Hoersholm

Grochowski M (2005) Powiązania Międzynarodowe Obszaru Metropolitalnego Warszawy [International Connectivity of the Warsaw Metropolitan Area]. Polska Akademia Nauk, Warsaw

Groth N B (ed) (2001) Cities and Networking: The Baltic Sea Region. Danish Forest and Landscape Research Institute, Hornsholm

IGEAT (= Institut de Gestion de l'Environment et d'Aménagement du Territoire, Université Libre de Bruxelles) (2006) Spatial Scenarios and Orientations in Relation to the ESDP and Cohesion Policy. Working Document. Scenario Report. IGEAT, Bruxelles

Jałowiecki B (2004) Czy Warszawa będzie metropolią europejską? [Will Warsaw become a European metropolis?]. In: Kukliński A (ed) Globalizacja Warszawy – strategiczny problem XXI wieku [Globalization of Warsaw – a Strategic Problem of the 21st Century]. Polskie Towarzystwo Współpracy z Klubem Rzymskim, Oficyna Wydawnicza 'Rewasz', Warsaw

Korcelli-Olejniczak E (2004) Funkcje metropolitalne Berlina i Warszawy w latach 1990-2002. Wspózależność pozycji w systemie miast Europy Środkowej [Metropolitan Functions of Berlin and Warsaw in the Period of 1990-2002. Interdependence of Positions in the Urban System of Central Europe]. Polska Akademia Nauk, Instytut Geografii i Przestrzennego Zagospodarowania im. Stanisława Leszczyckiego, Warsaw

Krätke S (2004) Ansatzpunkte zur Stärkung der Wirtschaftspotenziale Berlins. Vorlage für die Enquete-Kommission "Eine Zukunft für Berlin" [Ways of strengthening Berlin's economic potentials. Proposal for the commission "A Future for Berlin"]. Available online: http://www.kraetke.privat.t-online.de/Wirtschaftspotenziale-Enquetekommission.pdf, visited on 19.02.2007

Kujath H J (2005) Restructuring of the Metropolitan Region of Berlin-Brandenburg, Economic Trends and Political Answers. Geographia Polonica 78: 117–136

Kukliński A (2000) The Warsaw Metropolis and the Challenges of Globalization, In: Kukliński A (ed) The knowledge-based economy, 5. The European challenges of the 21st century. State Committee for Scientific Research, Warszawa, 240–261

Lichtenberger E (2000) Vienna – from Medieval Burger Town to Eurometropolis. In: Lichtenberger E (ed) Society and Regions. Austrian Academy of Sciences Press, Vienna, 319–333

Maastricht Treaty (1992). Available online: http://www.eurotreaties.com/maastrichtext.html, visited on 17.01.2006

Minichbauer R, Mitterdorfer E (2000) European Cultural Networks and Networking in Central and Eastern Europe. Available online: http://www.eipcp.net, visited on 20.04.2006.

Nordregio (= Nordic Centre for Spatial Development) (2004) Potentials for Polycentric Development in Europe. Final Report. Available online: http://www.espon.eu/mmp/online/website/content/projects/259/648/file_1174/fr-1.1.1_revised-full.pdf, visited on 19.02.2007

Schulman H, Kanninen V (2002) Urban Networking: Trends and Perspectives in the Baltic Sea Region. Geographia Polonica 75: 479–488

SFS (= Senatsverwaltung für Stadtentwicklung) (2004) Stadtentwicklungskonzept Berlin 2020 [Urban Development Concept Berlin 2020]. Kulturbuchverlag. Berlin

ZMSW (= Zarząd Miasta Stołecznego Warszawy) (2005) Strategia Rozwoju Miasta Stołecznego Warszawy do 2020 roku [The Strategy of Development of Warsaw until 2020]. Warszawa

IV Sectoral perspectives on border regions

Transborder transport

The case of Poland's present and future Schengen area boundaries

Tomasz Komornicki

Institute of Geography and Spatial Organization, Polish Academy of Sciences, Warsaw

1 Introduction

In the 19th and first half of the 20th centuries in Europe, there was a tendency to formalize boundaries. Its extreme form was the "iron curtain", which evolved from a strong military frontier into an economic and a social barrier. Many countries introduced their own standards in terms of transport infrastructure such as railway gauges or the mode of supplying electricity to railways. This tendency reverted with the onset of European integration processes.

Since the 1950s, national borders started to become permeable – from the Benelux countries towards Southern Europe and, after 1989, towards Eastern Europe, too. However, the increasing permeability of boundaries inside the integrating area often strengthens external borders. This is currently the case with the external borders of the European Union, such as Poland's eastern borders including the Polish-Ukrainian border.

The Schengen Convention was signed in 1990 and came into effect in 1995. It abolished checks at internal borders of the signatory countries and created a single external frontier, where checks for all Schengen signatories were to be carried out in accordance with a common set of rules. Currently, all EU-15 countries except Ireland and the United Kingdom have joined the convention, as well as Iceland and Norway. The 12 countries that entered the EU in 2004 and 2007 will join the Schengen Convention in 2008 at the earliest.

After EU enlargement in 2004, the number and length of borders between the European Union and third countries increased abruptly. Romania and Bulgaria having joined the EU since then, there are many more external boundaries with third countries such as Russia, Belarus, Ukraine, Turkey, Croatia, Macedonia, Serbia and Albania than before the latest two accession rounds. This process polarises European border regime systems. The formalization of borders inside the EU is decreasing while its new external borders are becoming increasingly formalized.

Pan-European cargo traffic has been increasing since 1989 owing to geopolitical changes and integration processes. The potential future limitation of mobility foreseen in strategic planning is often regarded as unrealistic in the face of the desire to strengthen the EU's competitiveness in the global economy (Banister et al. 2000).

Under these circumstances, boundaries have become the locus of conflicts between transport and the natural environment. This holds especially for border segments which were characterized by low permeability in the past. In such areas, valuable ecosystems were able to persist or newly develop. Nowadays they are subject to strong pressure from increasing border traffic and transport-related projects. For instance, nine of Poland's 23 national parks are directly adjacent to the national boundary and a further six are in the immediate vicinity of the boundary. However, permanent border congestion also impairs the environment.

The purpose of the present article is to document transformations that have taken place in the domain of transport infrastructure and cross-border traffic on 'new' (since 2004) internal and external boundaries of the European Union. In the first case, the Polish-German border is taken as an example and in the second the Polish-Ukrainian border. The latter became less permeable with the accession of Poland to the European Union. An examination of the situation on both boundaries is preceded by a theoretical introduction to transborder transport in Europe and a description of its development in Poland after 1989. Concluding remarks have been formulated from the standpoint of sustainability aims.

Transborder sustainability was treated firstly as the situation where the externalities of transport in the transborder section are not higher than inside neighbouring countries. From this point of view, the most important policy aims are to avoid congestion and shift cargo traffic from road to rail and intermodal transport. In a wider sense, policy could also seek generally to reduce the transport externalities caused by international mobility.

2 Transborder transport

The term "transborder transport" refers to transport infrastructure crossing political boundaries, as well as to cross-border passenger and goods traffic. Generally it is considered from three viewpoints, the primary study objects being:

a) transport,
b) boundary,
c) international interactions (as reflected by passenger and goods traffic).

(a) focuses on the functioning of the transborder transport infrastructure, (b) emphasises the political aspect, and (c) addresses the broader problem of the influence exerted by boundaries on the intensity of economic (e.g., foreign trade) and social linkages (e.g., migration or tourism), and on innovation diffusion.

The transborder transport infrastructure may constitute a part of the regular transportation network, or it may have a specific character. The former includes cross-border infrastructure such as roads, railways, pipelines, and waterways, as well as airports and seaports, while the latter includes facilities or network elements specifically related to cross-border functions such as passenger and cargo-handling border crossings, customs terminals, reloading stations, fee payment outlets, and truck weighing stations.

The impact of borders as barriers to transport depends on the degree of formalisation and on the degree of permeability. In addition, poorly permeable boundaries limit not only the transborder transport of persons and goods, but also network development. In extreme cases the infrastructure may even deteriorate. For instance, numerous transport routes crossing the borders of the former Soviet Union with its neighbours were not used over decades and have fallen into deliberate or natural disrepair.

In general terms, permeable boundaries are characterised by a low or even non-existing significance of the specific infrastructure and the intensive development of normal networks – up to the levels of density existing inside the individual countries. Currently there are practically no boundaries characterised by a very low degree of permeability in Europe. Weakly permeable borders display intensified investment in specific infrastructure. This infrastructure becomes a substitute for true permeability – bigger and modernized border crossings are potentially capable of serving thousands of persons and vehicles. Nevertheless gigantic queues arise in their vicinity owing to formal limitations such as detailed customs controls.

On a strongly formalised and weakly permeable boundary, the barrier effect is apparent first of all in the low intensity of transborder interactions. Liberalisation of the border regime in conjunction with the economic opening of neighbouring countries increases demand for international transport services. In such cases, the transboundary transport infrastructure proves insufficient. Routes crossing the borders become bottlenecks in the supra-national transport system. This took place, for instance, after 1990 at the borders of the European Union with the countries of Central Europe.

The phenomenon of border congestion has a direct economic aspect, especially with regard to the transport of goods. The solution consists in further liberalising the regime and even abolishing most border functions, as in the Schengen territory, and/or extension of the infrastructure. Numerous recent reports perceive boundaries not as demarcation lines but as evolving “mobile frontiers”. In such a perspective the barriers to transport have a temporary character. Their gradual reduction is envisaged in line with the processes of spatial integration (Corvers & Giaoutzi 1998).

The barrier effect of a boundary disturbs the flow of goods or passengers expected on the basis of the gravity models of trade – in conformity with normal resistance to distance. The regression line, representing the intensity of interaction along distance, “breaks” and dips at the distance corresponding to a political frontier. It was shown that this break also persists at very highly permeable boundaries, such as the internal boundaries of the European Union (Rietveld 2001) and even between some administrative units of a lower order (Lowe & Moryadas 1975). One of the main reasons is the ineratia of the interaction system. Local linkages based on previous economic sub-systems endure even after changes in border functions (Domański 1982).

Transborder transport may be local, regional or continental in nature. Transport of supra-national significance also takes place across boundaries of low permeability, while local transport most frequently reflects a mild border regime. Its development stimulates cross-border collaboration and economies of the border-adjacent regions.

3 Transborder transport in Poland

3.1 Overview

The functioning conditions of transportation infrastructure have undergone extreme changes since the beginning of the economic transformation in Poland. These changes have particularly affect areas adjacent to borders, where the earlier determinants of transport development of had often been military considerations, as well as the economic interests of third countries. With respect to the new conditions in which the transport infrastructure operates in the border zones of Poland, the following factors should be mentioned:

- Functional transformations of boundaries and the increase in cross-border traffic.
- Change of direction in the Polish foreign trade because the Soviet Union has been replaced by the unified Germany as the main trading partner.
- Change in the direction of transit movements, i.e., a decline in North-South transit and, after 2000, a relative decrease in the role of transit from the Russian direction. The significance of transit from Lithuania and other Baltic countries to Germany and Western Europe has steadily increased. There is also a general upward trend in Ukrainian transit volume.
- Accession to the European Union in 2004 and integration into the network of European transport corridors as well as the improved opportunities to finance investment projects through European funds.

On average, a hard surface road with or without a checkpoint crosses the national border of Poland every 22 km. The densest network of transboundary roads exists along the boundary with the Kaliningrad District of the Russian Federation. There is one hard surface road per 12 km of this particular border. The boundary with the Kaliningrad District, established in 1945, divided the former Eastern Prussia, which had existed as an economic organism for several centuries. The situation along the border with the Czech Republic is also advantageous, with one road per 14 km. The average distance between transborder roads at the Polish-German border is 21 km. The poorest border accessibility by road is along Poland's border with Slovakia, with one road per 35 km of the boundary line. This is largely because the border follows the Carpathian Mountains. The main reason for the low density of roads crossing the border with Ukraine – one per 48 km – is the low level of infrastructure development in the Eastern part of pre-war Poland (see fig. 1).

The degree to which the transboundary infrastructure is used can be measured

- by the share of roads on which there are any – or only generally accessible – border crossings, and
- by the percentage of railways with border crossings – or railways with scheduled passenger services.

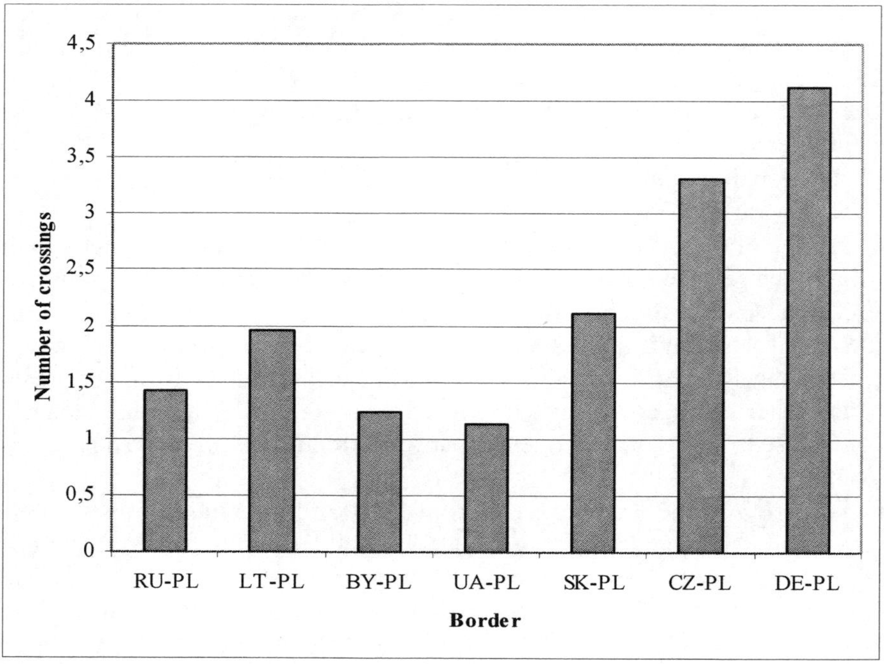

Figure 1. Number of generally accessible border crossings per 100 km

In contrast to the endowment of boundaries with transport infrastructure, the use of this infrastructure increased considerably in between 1989 and 2002 (Komornicki 2004). For all the land boundaries of Poland the percentage of transboundary hard surface roads with generally accessible border crossings increased from 30% to 48% from 1993 to 1997 alone. The greatest use is made of the transboundary road network crossing the Polish-German border. Border crossings are on the existing relevant hard surface roads increased from 68% in 1993 to 86% in 1997.

By far the least use is made of the road infrastructure on the border with the Kaliningrad District – only 17%. The degree of infrastructure use is somewhat higher for the rail network, where the average for all boundaries is close to 75%. A vast majority are used for cargo transport. Passenger services operate across borders on exactly half the transboundary lines – 22 out of 44.

In terms of numbers and accessibility of border crossings, the situation on the Polish western and southern boundaries is close to saturation point because the majority of regional and local centres in border regions have connections with cities or towns in neighbouring countries. Along the border with the Czech Republic and Slovakia, numerous border crossings, accessible until quite recently only for local traffic, have been made available for general purposes. In recent years, pedestrian border crossings as well as those for tourist traffic have also been opened. On the eastern border, many new facilities have been constructed from scratch. The remaining crossings have been completely overhauled, partly funded by the European Union with the aim of tightening the eastern border of the Union. For instance, a large customs terminal has been established on the Warsaw-Moscow route. Still, the eastern boundary of Poland is traversed by numerous transport routes with no border crossing function. The sense of establishing these crossings is still conditional on the future degree of permeability of the eastern boundary of the European Union.

Between 1990 and1997, passenger cross-border traffic in both directions increased in Poland from 84.2 million to 273.9 million (Komornicki 1999). This increase was followed by stagnation. In the years 2000 and 2001 passenger traffic even decreased. Traffic was dominated by short shopping trips to Poland. In 2003 a total of 181 million persons crossed the borders in both directions. In 2004, though, there was again an increase, associated with Poland's accession to the EU. This increase took place across all the border segments except those with Russia and Belarus. On the majority of the border segments, foreigners account for most cross-border traffic. This is most pronounces at local Polish-German border crossings in the vicinity of bazaars, and at the borders with Belarus and Ukraine. At some border crossings on the eastern borders, the share of Polish citizens crossing the boundary does not exceed 5%. Among the people registered at airports and on the Czech and Slovak borders, however, Poles dominate.

The dynamic increase in the intensity of heavy goods vehicles (HGV) traffic continued throughout the decade and to the present day. In 1980 all Polish borders were crossed in both directions by a total of 295,000 HGVs. By 1990, this number had increased to 1.1 million, and by 2003 to almost 6.2 million. During the entire decade the dominating role was played by lorry traffic across the Polish-German border (see fig. 2).

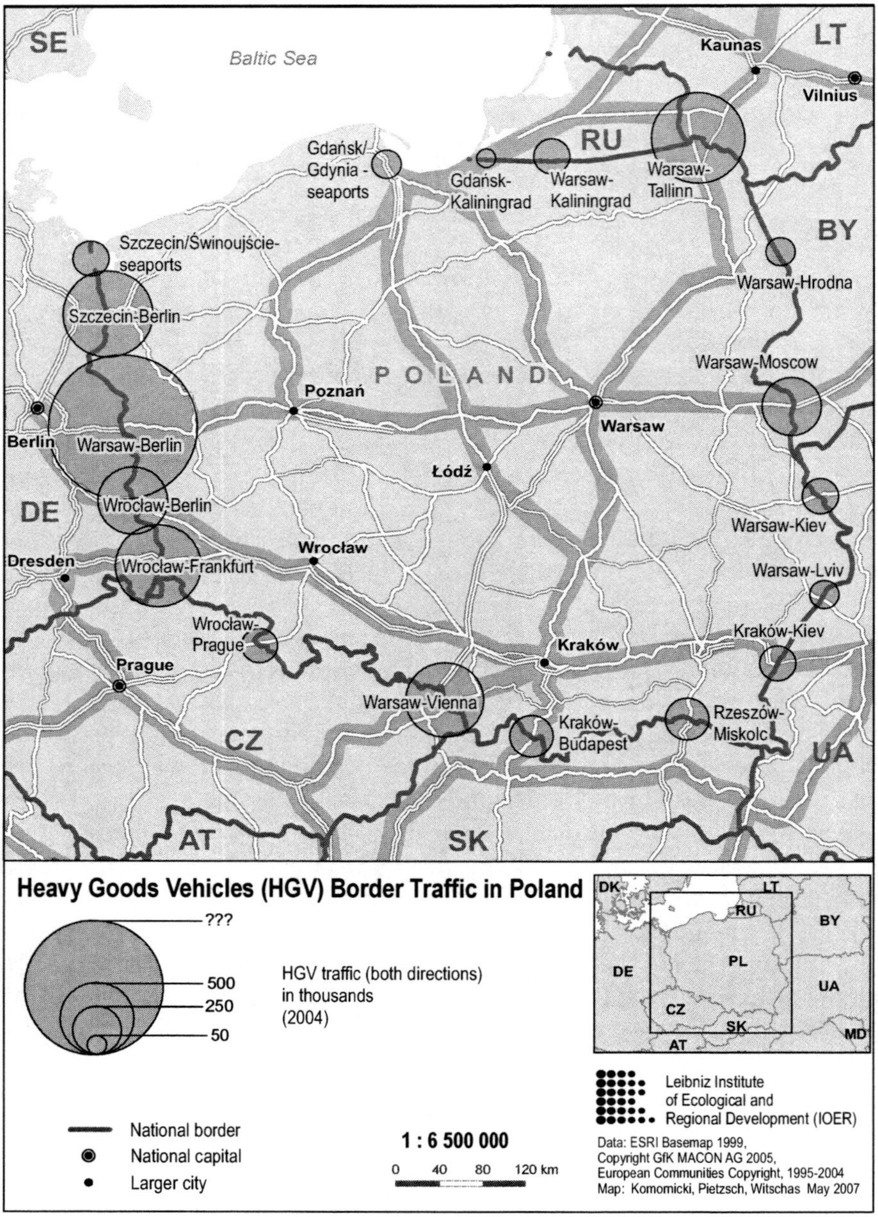

Figure 2. Heavy Goods Vehicles (HGV) Border Traffic in Poland

3.2 The Polish-German border

The Polish-German border is crossed by two pan-European transport corridors determined by the European Conference of the Ministers of Transport (ECMT) at the meeting on Crete in 1994:

- Corridor II – Berlin-Moscow and
- Corridor III – Berlin-Kiev, with the branching of Dresden-Wrocław.

In addition, the subsequent ECMT meeting in Helsinki in 1997, the southern corridor Świnoujście-Prague, currently referred as the central European transport corridor, was designated as a potential pan-European corridor.

The present situation as to the number and accessibility of border crossings appears to be close to saturation point. During the period of transformation, all older facilities have been modernised, and, in addition, two large border crossings for cargo traffic have been opened on the motorway from Wrocław to Dresden and on a national highway southeast of Berlin, as well as seven local crossings. In recent years several new pedestrian border crossings have also been established along with crossing points for minor border traffic. These projects involved the construction or reconstruction of six bridges across the border rivers Nysa/Neisse and Odra/Oder.

While many local and regional railway lines have been closed down, several main lines have been modernized. The latter include the line Warsaw-Poznań-Berlin and the line Wrocław-Zgorzelec(-Dresden). Travel time from Warsaw to Berlin has essentially been reduced from almost 10 hours in the early 1990s to 5 hours and 40 minutes at the present time. Yet this is still relatively long considering the distance is less than 600 km. This is particularly due to the need to change electric locomotives (different electricity supply systems) and the high number of level crossing junctions with the road network, imposing lower speeds. Despite modernisation, the Wrocław-Dresden line is used far less intensively than in the past. Long-distance passenger train connections on this line have even been suspended.

There are several examples of railway border crossings newly established in the 1990s on lines that had not been used previously or used only for cargo transport. Such a border crossing has been opened with success in Kostrzyn (PL)/Küstrin (D) north-east of Berlin.

During last ten to fifteen years, efforts have been undertaken on several occasions to organize combined rail and road transport in Polish-German transborder relations. However, the service offered was generally not competitive enough for the operators even at times when many hours of waiting in queues at the border was an everyday experience. The promotion of such intermodal modes of cargo transport appears to be a key element in the policy of sustainable transport in the border zone.

The yearly number of crossings at the Polish-German border increased very fast in the first half of the 1990s as near-border trade developed intensively. In the peak period between 1994 and 1999, traffic in both directions exceeded 130 million person-crossings a year. This traffic was clearly dominated by Germans who had a share of almost 70% (Kormornicki 1999).

After 1999, traffic declined in intensity because the retail price gap between Poland and Germany narrowed and because large shopping malls on the German side of the border began to compete with Polish bazaars. As a result, the trading activity of Poles decreased. However, this tendency has stopped since Poland's accession to the EU in May 2004. At local crossings, especially if situated in the vicinity of small communities, German citizens distinctly predominate. At crossings on main transit routes, Poles prevail. These crossings also concentrate traffic of third country citizens.

Polish-German HGV traffic increased throughout the period 1990–2003. This is due to the continuous intensification of bilateral economic ties, but partly also to increased transit between other, more distant locations.

3.3 The Polish-Ukrainian border

At the beginning of the 1990s, there was only one road border crossing at Medyka and one railway crossing at Przemyśl. Other railway crossings had been reserved for cargo traffic. There were also seldom used crossings for the so-called "simplified cross-border traffic" governed by the Polish-Soviet agreement which was finally annulled along when visas where introduced.

From 1993 on, several new border crossings were installed. As they came into operation border traffic de-concentration increased. New border crossings also generated additional traffic, encouraging the inhabitants of the areas adjacent to the borderto engage in petty trade.

Polish-Ukrainian border traffic recorded extremely dynamic growth in terms of both persons and vehicles in the first half of the 1990s. Person traffic reached a first peak in 1991, when the border was crossed in both directions by almost 7.4 million persons. At this time Ukraine was still a part of the Soviet Union. This was the period just after the border had been opened for mass traffic. Price hikes in Poland, resulting from the transition to the free market economy, made petty trade attractive. This trade involved importing cheap products from the collapsing Soviet economy and selling them on Polish bazaars.

The subsequent years, though, brought a slow decrease of traffic intensity. The primary cause was the worsening of the economic situation in Ukraine due to the separation from Russia and the initiation of economic reforms. The price of consumption goods in Ukraine increased significantly. At the same time, the situation in Poland was already gradually improving and the number of bazaar customers decreased.

1994–1997 was again a period of an intensive traffic increases, mostly, involving foreigners. The direction of cross-border trade changed. Ukrainians started to visit Poland to do their shopping there. The second dip in traffic intensity took place in 1998 owing to the Russian economic crisis, which encompassed the entire area of the former Soviet Union, and partly also owing to the introduction of the Polish aliens act. Traffic dwindled to the level of 1995.

Another wave of development in cross-border trade occurred in 1999–2001. Simultaneously, there was a renewed increase in the number of Poles travelling to Ukraine. In 2001 the border was crossed in both directions by the record number of almost 12 million persons.

These trend figures refer only to road crossings. Traffic at railway crossings has been decreasing steadily since the early 1990s. Poles are using rail transport to a greater extent. The Ukrainians who come to Poland to shop mainly come by car or coach. For Poles the train border queues to be avoided.

Analysis of the intensity of cross-border person traffic reveals a characteristic seasonal cycle with a distinct summer maximum and a drop in the winter months. This cycle was disturbed by a drop associated with introduction of visas on October 1, 2003. The delay, after which traffic fluctuations of returned to the earlier rhythm was, however, quite short. Already in December 2003, the intensity of border traffic had returned to the level of the preceding year. Starting in March 2004, though, both Ukrainians and Poles returned to the typical spring increase in mobility among. The date of May 1, 2004, i.e., of the accession of Poland to the European Union, has not exerted any influence on existing trends in this domain.

HGV traffic at the Polish-Ukrainian border increased without interruption between 1990 and 1997. In 1998–1999 there was a short reduction, followed by continued rapid intensification.

The opening of subsequent border crossings resulted not only in the de-concentration of goods traffic. There were also "shifts" of traffic between crossings, associated with the lengths of queues, severity of inspections, or installation of control facilities, especially vehicle weighing. HGV traffic also undergoes standard seasonal fluctuations with a clear peak at the end of the calendar year and an even more pronounced minimum in January. The introduction of visas for Ukrainians has had no perceptible influence on the intensity of traffic. The spring increase in 2004 came earlier than in the preceding year, which suggests either that Polish accession to the European Union had no influence on the magnitude of traffic, or that this impact could be positive.

4 Conclusions – towards sustainable transborder transport

The period of a spontaneous development in transborder transport at Poland's external borders between 1990 and 2000 exerted a negative influence on the natural environment of border-adjacent areas. This was primarily due to

- modal shifts in transport, expressed as a shift from railway to road transport,
- intensified car traffic on roads in border areas which had until then been neglected in terms of investment,
- congestion at border crossings which generated increased emissions as well as environmental degradation in the immediate vicinity of roads and border crossings,
- unfavourable regulations imposed to meet customs policy requirements such as a ban on crossing the Polish-Russian, Polish-Belarusian and Polish-Ukrainian borders on foot, except for one crossing.

In the period after 2000, the road infrastructure was ameliorated and border queues were reduced. This mitigated some of the negative tendencies mentioned above.

With Poland's accession to the EU on 1 May 2004, customs inspections were abolished at the borders to other EU Member States. In practice This eliminated border congestion. Even before accession, local and regional governments made use of European structural funds to construct by-passes, pedestrian border crossings and transborder bicycle paths, which helped to improve the ecological situation in border areas.

At the same time, congestion persists, especially in goods traffic, at Poland's new EU-external border. This is largely dependent on the effectiveness of border services in neighbouring countries.

Beyond any doubt, the most important task in balancing the ecological costs of developing transborder transport infrastructure is now to stimulate intermodal transport in cargo traffic. This applies equally to the EU's internal and external boundaries. It seems realistic to think about redressing the role of transborder passenger railway transport over the main routes, provided they are adapted to high speed traffic, and locally in transborder tourist zones. The proportionality of international train fares is also important. For instance, a single train ticket from Warsaw to Berlin is still more expensive than two domestic tickets put together and crossing the border on foot. The continued construction of by-pass roads around border towns also helps minimize the negative influence of road transport.

Whether Poland and other new EU Member States join the Schengen Convention will have a significant influence on traffic intensity across the new internal boundaries of the EU and the spatial effects of this traffic. If these countries join the convention, all the inspection posts along the borders will be eliminated and there will be no restrictions whatsoever for crossing the border at any location. Against this background it is pointless to modernise existing border facilities now. The increase in traffic may, on the other hand, the transborder transport infrastructure to be extended to deal with for pedestrians and cyclists, too.

The possibility of crossing the border at any point may entail local hazards to natural environment. For Poland the borders with the Czech Republic and Slovakia are particularly affected, and to a lesser degree the river border with Germany. It will become necessary to limit road traffic in accordance with the road codes of neighbouring countries. Car traffic will have to be prohibited on forest and mountain roads.

On the other hand, the total lifting of all forms of border control should have a positive impact from the sustainability point of view by eliminating the congestion problem. Negative impacts from a general increase of traffic could be registered in Europe as a whole, but will be not concentrated in internal border areas. Generally speaking, post-enlargement transborder trends in transport are positive at borders between EU Member States and negative at the external boundaries.

References

Banister D, Stead D, Steen P, Akerman J, Dreborg K, Nijkamp P, Schleicher-Tappeser R (2000) European Transport Policy and Sustainable Mobility. Spon Press, London, New York

Corvers F, Giaoutzi M (1998) Borders and Barriers and Changing Opportunities for Border Regional Development. In: Button K, Nijkamp P, Priemus H (eds) Transport Networks in Europe. Concepts, Analysis and Policies. Edward Elgar Publishing, Cheltenham, 291–306

Domański R (1982) Teoretyczne podstawy geografii ekonomicznej [Theoretical basis of Economic Geography]. PWE, Warszawa

Komornicki T (1999) Granice Polski. Analiza zmian przenikalności w latach 1990–1996 [Boundaries of Poland. Analysis of changes in permeability in the years 1990-1996]. IGiPZ PAN, Warszawa

Komornicki T (2004) Impact of border regime institutions on transport network development in Central and Eastern Europe. In: Rietveld P, Stough RR (eds) Barriers to Sustainable Transport. Institutions, Regulation and sustainability. Spon Press, London, New York, 183–196

Lowe JC, Moryadas S (1975) The Geography of Movement. Boston: Houghton Mifflin.

Rietveld P (2001) Obstacles to openness of border regions in Europe. In: Geenhuizen M, Ratti R (eds) Gaining Advantage from Open Borders. An active space approach to regional development. Ashgate, Aldershot, 79–96

Sustainable tourism development in cross-border biosphere reserves of Central and Eastern Europe

Birgit Nolte

Institute for Geography, University of Greifswald

1 Introduction

All over Europe, a paradigm change in protected areas and nature protection has been arisen. The new role combines nature conservation with the promotion of regional development. Consequently, large protected areas gain additional functions, for example as tools for regional development. Especially for areas located on borders, trans-boundary activities are very important to attain these goals.

The situation in Central and Eastern Europe differs from that in Western Europe because of the transformation process that has consequences for every area of life. In addition, accession to the European Union has led to new regulatory framework conditions to which national legislation has had to be adapted, e.g., with regard to the EU Habitats Directive. Furthermore, tourists are increasingly discovering sensitive areas that have developed nearly untouched for several decades, many in border regions. In other words, the growing market for nature-oriented tourism is exerting growing pressure on sensitive areas. The tourism patterns have also changed, e.g., more often but shorter holidays and more diverse tourist demands.

This article describes and analyses the situation of selected Central and Eastern European biosphere reserves in border regions as a special type of protected area. The concept of biosphere reserves is very promising though their implementation is challenging for a region. Two cross-border regions were examined with regard to sustainable tourism development, as it is a part of the international concept of biosphere reserves:

- Bohemian-Bavarian Forest astride the border between the Czech Republic and Germany and Czech Republic; and
- the Karst region spanning the border between Hungary and Slovakia (see fig. 1).

The case studies focus on experience with implementing the sustainability concept as well as with trans-boundary cooperation. The findings are based on literature surveys, document analyses, and semi-structured interviews with key actors in the studied regions.

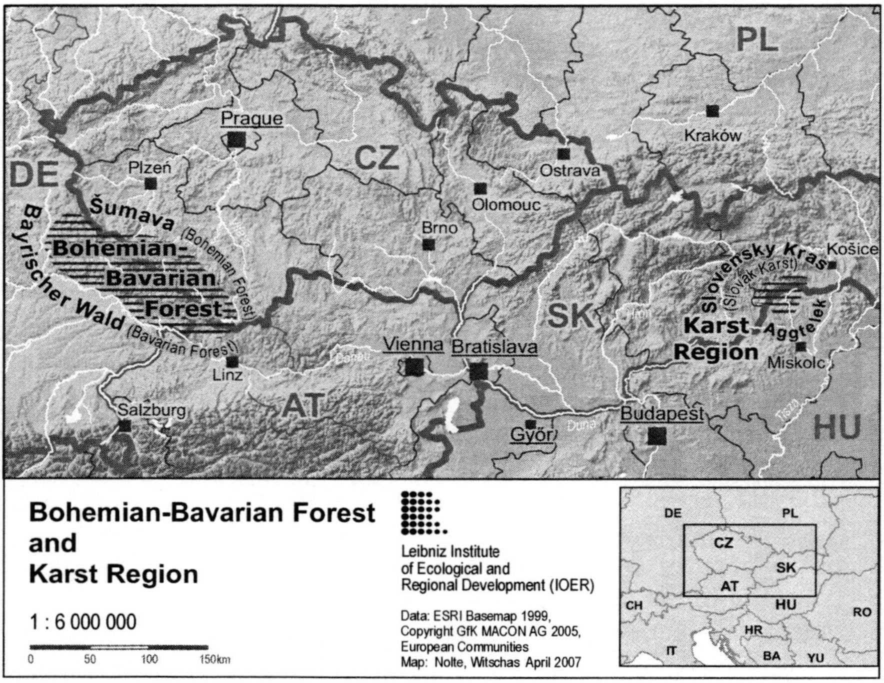

Figure 1. Bohemian-Bavarian Forest and Karst Region

2 Biosphere reserves as special places

2.1 Paradigm shift in nature protection

The function of protected areas – especially in the case of large protected areas – has changed over recent decades. The new approach tries to combine nature conservation with the promotion of regional development. By contrast, the traditional approach emphasises the protection of nature against human impacts. Initially, nature protection always implied separating natural landscape and areas under use. Since the 1970s, the opinion that protection of nature without human agency could not be efficient, was more and more commonly accepted. Contemporary nature protection places greater emphasis on the integrative aspects and on the networking concept in combination with human involvement (see table 1).

Table 1. Traditionally preserving versus dynamic and innovative approaches to nature conservation (Weixlbaumer 1998)

Traditionally preserving approach to nature conservation	Dynamic and innovative approach to nature conservation
Separation of nature protection areas and areas under use	Integrating basic principle in regard to space and time
Sectoral protection	Holistic principle, sustainable development
Mainly protection of land	Protection of land as well as protection of processes
Management: secondary role	Management: primary role
Top-down	(Social objective) "top-down" and "bottom-up"
Strictly regulated, normative	Voluntary
Acceptance by stakeholders not important	Acceptance by stakeholders should be considered
Nature and humankind as contradiction	Nature and humankind as entity

To date, the traditionally preserving approach is being replaced by more dynamic and innovative forms of nature protection. In consequence, the recent establishment of new protected areas is often connected with the new role as tools for regional development. As many case studies in Europe show, large protected areas can contribute actively to regional development and can be used as tools to promote economic growth and protect biodiversity.

In the countries of Central and Eastern Europe, this discussion is not as lively as in Western Europe. The traditional opinion that protected areas chiefly have to preserve nature and protect it from human impact is widely held. Additionally, nature protection is often seen as inhibiting economic activities. EU-legislation such as the Environmental Impact Assessment

Directive and the Birds Directive are perceived as obstacles to economic growth.

A good example of the overall paradigm shift in nature protection is the establishment of a specific type of large protected area: the biosphere reserve.

2.2 International concept of biosphere reserves

The concept of biosphere reserve is an essential part of the "Man and the Biosphere Programme" (MAB) of the United Nation Environmental, Scientific and Educational Organization (UNESCO). In 1976 the first biosphere reserves were designated. Biosphere reserves are supposed to fulfil three functions (UNESCO 2002: 17):

- Conservation – to protect those genetic resources, species, ecosystems and landscapes which require protection.
- Development – to foster sustainable economic and human development compatible with the first function.
- Logistic function - to facilitate demonstration projects, environmental education and training, research and monitoring.

Until the beginning of the 1990s, the conservation and logistic functions dominated, with the development role left rather undefined. During that period, the goal to establish a network of representative examples of the world's ecosystem predominated. This was driven by the idea of worldwide networking and the exchange of experience and scientific research. At any rate, the importance of integrated approaches was already recognized at the international level and in the framework of the MAB programme. The concept proposes a simple generalized zoning pattern for biosphere reserves, combining

- a core zone with highest biodiversity and protection,
- a buffer zone for education, research and some tourism-related facilities, and
- a transition zone with settlements, tourism and extensive land-use.

The turning point was marked by the Seville Conference in 1995, where the concept was reviewed and re-defined. The repercussions of the United Nation Conference on Environment and Development in Rio de Janeiro in 1992 led to a stronger emphasis on sustainable development and its implementation in biosphere reserves. Thus the concept was focused on the development function. Its character as a holistic approach became more apparent. The 1995 Seville Strategy defines sustainability as an integrated concept of conservation combining the preservation of ecological diversity with research, environmental monitoring and education. Biosphere reserves are designated and managed with the objective of promoting and combining biodiversity conservation with sustainable development based on community participation and science. The objective of a biosphere reserve is to achieve a balance between the often conflicting goals of conserving biological diversity and promoting human development while maintaining associated cultural values. They are 'spaces for reconciling people and nature' (UNESCO 2002: 6).

2.3 Implementations of the biosphere reserve concept in East Central Europe

National perceptions of the international biosphere reserve concept depend on – among other things – how it has been implemented in the given country. The legal status of biosphere reserves therefore differs from country to country. In Germany, biosphere reserves are a special category in national environmental legislation. In Slovakia, by contrast, they are not mentioned in the law since biosphere reserves their primary purpose is nature conservation and protection to the exclusion of human activities. Consequently, the international status has little impact on the area and on national land-use regulations. In other words, the potential legal and other consequences of biosphere reserve status are overruled by national protection categories such as national park and protected landscape area. Few local or regional stakeholders see the concept of biosphere reserve as a tool for regional sustainable development. At the national level, nature conservation is linked to traditional objectives such as preservation of the natural landscape.

In many cases, national concepts of nature protection in Central and Eastern Europe are still rooted in the past socialist systems. At that time, industrial development was concentrated in urban areas, which meant that the undisturbed development of ecosystems was possible outside these centres; for example at national borders or in peripheral areas that were unsuitable for industrial production. In these areas, natural landscapes could develop nearly without human impact and the biodiversity of plants and animals was growing.

Of the political regime change of 1989/1990 has had profound consequences for nature protection. Pollution in general is declining, especially water and air pollution. But the diversity of species and the preservation of strictly protected areas are increasingly endangered by unsustainable exploitation, land-use changes, increasing traffic, river regulation, and the growing consumption of land. Accession to the EU in 2004 has further promoted the idea of market liberalisation, but this also contributes to serious threats for biodiversity. Tourism development in peripheral areas is another recently emerging threat to biodiversity.

Regional case studies in four biosphere reserves have shown that the biosphere reserve concept is not being sufficiently implemented in Central and Eastern Europe (Nolte 2005), although the authorities in charge of biosphere reserves are often committed to sustainable development and cooperation with regional stakeholders. However, these ambitions generally are poorly communicated. Even though the goals of sustainable development are fixed on paper, in practice there is not enough commitment to implement these ideas by, for example, motivating the local population to actively take part in this process.

2.4 Cross-border cooperation within the framework of biosphere reserves

Cross-border collaboration is crucial to the development of the world network of biosphere reserves. Good examples are the setting-up of trans-boundary reserves and the promotion of other forms of cross-border cooperation such as 'twinning' arrangements between two reserves in different countries or cooperation between reserves in particular geographic regions.

The benefits of this kind of cooperation can be summarized as follows (EUROPARC Federation 2001; Sandwith et al. 2001):

- more effective management of natural resources and natural systems,
- preservation and enhancement of local cultures,
- promotion of the economic welfare of a region's communities and
- reduction in political tensions and promotion of peace.

In the framework of UNESCO's MAB programme, trans-frontier cooperation has increased since the Seville Strategy was adopted in 1995 because it is emphasised in this document. Networking is one of the most important factors for biosphere reserves. Only seven trans-boundary biosphere reserves have been officially registered to date in the MAB network (UNESCO 2006).

3 Case studies of two cross-border regions with biosphere reserves

The following case studies provide insight into the situation of two border regions with four biosphere reserves:

- The Hungarian-Slovakian Karst region with the biosphere reserves Aggtelek (Hungary) and Slovensky Kras (Slovakia) and
- the Bohemian-Bavarian Forest with the biosphere reserves Bavarian Forest (Germany) and Bohemian Forest[13] (Czech Republic).

3.1 General description of the case study areas

3.1.1 The Slovak-Hungarian Karst region

The Karst region includes the two biosphere reserves – which are also national parks – Slovensky Kras in South East Slovakia and Aggtelek in North Hungary. The region is famous for its diverse karst phenomena. A series of plateaus, ranging from 400 to 900 m above sea level, are surrounded by steep slopes descending to adjacent basins, valleys and gorges. The region boasts of various dripstone caves, e.g., caves filled with ice and aragonite caves. Additionally, high biodiversity can be found, for instance a high number of butterfly and bat species. Therefore it is not astonishing that nature protection has a long tradition here. Slovensky Kras (Slovakia) as well as Aggtelek had already achieved protected landscape area statusin the late 1970s. Aggtelek became a national park in 1984 whereas in Slovensky Kras the national park was established only in 2002. One predominant factor is the difference in size between the two biosphere reserves. Aggtelek with nearly 20,000 hectares is only one third of the area of Slovensky Kras with a similar landscape and biodiversity features.

The character of the landscape differs in the two parts. In Hungary, subsistence agriculture and a typical rural village life dominates the picture. In Slovakia the region has an industrial-rural character with industries exploiting and processing raw materials, machinery and heavy metal industry in the vicinity of the protected area. In consequence, we can find two distinct expressions of structural economic weakness.

Despite the good cultural and natural prerequisites for tourism activities, tourism does not play an important role in the Karst region today. Visitors have come to the area since electrification of the Domica cave in 1932. It belongs to a greater cave system, which extents to over 25 km underground. In 2002, the Domica cave (Slovakia) had nearly 20,000 visitors. Tourism intensity on the Hungarian side is much higher. The Baradla cave had 150,000 visitors in 2002 and also a long tourist tradition because it is very famous in Hungary. In addition, historic places are interesting for visitors, e.g., the baroque castle of Betliar with more than 50,000 visitors in 2002. In sum, there are three main tourist activities in the Karst region

---

[13] In Czech the Bohemian Forest is called 'Sumava'.

(a) cave visiting, (b) visiting of cultural sites (Slovak castles), and (c) nature-orientated activities like hiking and biking.

Short-term tourism dominates in the region owing to the vicinity of Slovakia's second largest city, Kosice (240,000 inhabitants), which is the main source of visitors in the Slovak part. In Aggtelek, short-term tourism also predominates because tourists mostly make day trips to the region while staying overnight in other places such as the Hungarian city of Miscolc (180,000 inhabitants). Incoming tourism in both biosphere reserves is very weak, only 10% of visitors came from abroad. Therefore cross-border tourism is chiefly restricted to day trips.

In sum, the whole region is more of a local recreation and leisure area than an international tourism destination. Moreover, there is plainly no common tourism marketing or concept for the whole Karst region despite a common landscape and the highly attractive dripstone cave system.

The Slovak-Hungarian Karst region features the following *strengths* in terms of tourism development:

- Especially in Hungary the caves are well known.
- The cultural and natural attractions draw tourists.
- The supply of beds is sufficient for current tourist numbers.
- Positive information about the region is provided by the tourist information centre in Roznava and the national park administration in Aggtelek.

However, tourism development has *weaknesses*, too:

- Little money has been invested in tourism with the consequence that most beds are of a low standard.
- Little information about the biosphere reserve is being disseminated.
- Most visitors stay Moreno longer than 2 days.
- Tourism depends strongly on the summer season (July and August).

3.1.2 The Czech-German Bohemian-Bavarian Forest region

The Bohemian-Bavarian Forest region consists of the biosphere reserve Bohemian Forest in the western Czech Republic and the national park Bavarian Forest in south-eastern Germany. The Bohemian-Bavarian Forest also has a common border with Austria, but there are no large protected areas on the Austrian side. Thanks to its geographical position, the region kept its natural character to a large extent until the middle of the 20th century. It became well known for wood processing and glass making. Related settlements as well as resource exploitation have changed the landscape only slowly over recent centuries.

After World War II, the 'Iron Curtain' was established between the Czechoslovakian Socialist Republic and the Federal Republic of Germany, so that for over 40 years the area was dominated by the military, with severe consequences especially for Czech inhabitants. For instance, villages were destroyed and people were forced to leave the region. Consequently, the two parts of the Bohemian-Bavarian Forest developed in different ways, also in terms of tourism. The geographical situation at the border between East and West reinforced the economic marginality and the rural character of the whole region. On the other hand, it has helped to sustain natural attractions and to establish protected areas.

The region of the Bohemian-Bavarian Forest includes the largest forest complex in Central Europe. Due to its situation within densely populated Central Europe, its diversity in wildlife and its rich water resources, the region is often referred to as "the green roof of Europe". Typical for the landscape are spruce forests, peat bogs, meadows and altitudes varying between 1,378m and 490m above sea level (Valenta 1994; Tesitel et al. 2003; Evans & Henry 1995).

The Bavarian forest was declared the first national park in Germany as long ago as 1970. But also large parts of the Bohemian Forest have been put under conservation as protected landscape areas since 1963. Concerted efforts by nature conservationists led to the most vulnerable areas being declared as Bohemian Forest National Park in 1991. The German was designated a biosphere reserve in 1981 for and the Czech part in 1990 for. There are big differences in the size of the area: the Bavarian forest covers an area that is not even 10% of the area of the Bohemian Forest.

Due to the political situation, the parts of the region developed in different ways, and even today the effects of the past are still obvious in the tourism sector. The Bavarian Forest has a long tradition in tourism. Beginning in the 1960s, growing numbers of tourists visited the national park region mainly for hiking and cultural activities. For a number of years now, tourist numbers have remained constant but still at a high level of 2 million visitors per year. The tourism infrastructure is thus well established.

In the Bohemian Forest region, far-reaching changes occurred in the beginning of the 1990s. With the fall of the Iron Curtain, people could enter areas untouched for decades. Tourism developed rapidly but, because of the size of the area, there were local and seasonal differences. This has resulted in heterogeneous accommodation structures: ski-resorts and big hotels, but also private accommodation, small pensions, cheap cottages, and big campsites. Almost the same numbers of tourists visit the Bohemian Forest biosphere reserve (1.8 million) as the German Bavarian Forest biosphere reserve, but dispersed in an area ten times as large.

In both parts of the Bohemian-Bavarian Forest, domestic tourists have a 90% share. Economically, the villages on the German side depend heavily on tourism, as do some villages in the Bohemian Forest close to the German border.

The Bohemian-Bavarian Forest region features the following *strengths* in terms of tourism development:

- Long tradition of tourism (Germany) and dynamic growth in tourism respectively (Czech Republic).
- Good tourist infrastructure
- Average lengths of stay of 1–2 weeks, 1.8 million visitors per year, over 90% domestic tourism.
- Activities: mountain biking - especially in the Bohemian Forest, hiking, downhill and cross-country skiing.
- Protected areas have strong influence on tourism development.
- However, tourism development has *weaknesses*, too:
- In the Bavarian Forest: occupancy rates are low.
- In the Bohemian Forest: lack of a tourism organisation that could represent the interests of tourism stakeholders.
- In the Bohemian Forest regional consciousness is weak in contrast to the self-confidence of the Bavarian inhabitants regarding their landscape.

3.2 Role of protected area administrations

Administration in all four biosphere reserves suffers from a lack of personnel or public administrative entity concerned exclusively with the reserves. The scope for action differs extremely between the biosphere reserves under study.

In the Karst region, there are extraordinary administrative differences between biosphere reserves. In Aggtelek, Hungary, the administration is at the same time the regional authority for nature conservation. It also acts as a tour operator required to earn over 40% of its budget itself. This is only possible because the main attractions – the dripstone caves – are in the ownership of the national park itself. Besides managing the caves, they own a restaurant, a hotel and a campsite. They also organise tourist activities such as a village walk or horse riding. The national park is a strong trademark for tourism in the region.

In Slovakia, in contrast, the caves are managed by the national authority for caves, which has its office outside the region. Furthermore, the Slovak national park is authorized only to address nature conservation issues. The Slovensky Kras biosphere reserve became a national park only in 2002. This was followed by crucial changes in the administration such as the installation of a new director and an increase in staff. For the future it is promising that the Slovak administration became a more and more equal partner for the administration in Aggtelek.

Moreover, some recognition that the Hungarian biosphere reserve can be an engine for regional development is in evidence, but has so far gained little ground. The national park Aggtelek is, in fact, the main actor in the region. The two villages situated inside the national park function as centres for regional development and economic growth for the broader region on the Hungarian side.

The two partner administrations in the Bohemian-Bavarian Forest region are unequal. The Bohemian Forest National Park in the Czech Republic is an economically important stakeholder in the region because of its activities in wood processing and forestry, and provides employment for 340 workers. The administration themselves see their task more in the management of the national park. The biosphere reserve has a more theoretic character, combining the national park with the surrounded protected landscape area. The concept of the biosphere reserve as integrating economic growth and nature protection needs is not a topic in the everyday work of the administration. They see their task in tourism management and visitor guidance but not in tourism development. On the other side of the border, the Bavarian Forest administration concentrates on environmental education and tourism management in the area of the national park. Moreover, they are also important stakeholders for regional development. For instance, there are regular meetings with the national park administration and local authorities.

In addition, there are differences regarding regional identity. Experts claim that the Bohemian Forest has a relatively strong regional identity despite the long period in which it was dominated by the Iron Curtain. Due to exchanges of population after World War II, the family roots of many Czech inhabitants do not lie in that region. The situation in the Bavarian Forest is the contrary: many people have lived in this area for generations. The border that divides the Bohemian-Bavarian Forest into a Czech and a German part is still very strong in terms of culture and mentality, and with regard to the low intensity of cross-border interactions (Nolte 2005).

Slovensky Kras and Aggtelek have a common history. Before World War II, this area was a Hungarian district. The name from this time is still in common use: *Gömör Torna Karst*. On the Slovak side, the strong Hungarian minority identifies itself very much with this region and its Hungarian history.

Despite the differences between and inside the regions, the administrations are the driving forces cross-border cooperation.

3.3 Trans-boundary cooperation between biosphere reserves

Existing trans-border cooperation in the studied regions has to be seen in a historical context. Until 1990, trans-boundary cooperation, where it existed, was mainly an exchange of findings from scientific research. After regime change, international cooperation increased. Today it is one of the most important tasks of the administrations of the protected areas in both regions.

In the Karst region, the administrative staff of the Aggtelek and Slovensky Kras parks consider cooperation across the border to be very important. There are several projects, especially in the field of nature conservation. One recent project financed by the United Nations Environment Programme (UNEP) brings together different actors from the whole Karst region in the field of regional development. In the tourism sector, cooperation is weak. The Aggtelek National Park lists some Slovak accommodation in their tourism brochures but the overall tourism activities of the Slovensky Kras administration are marginal. The highlight of international activities was designation as a world heritage site in 1995. Despite this sobering situation, the Europarc Federation (2001: 77) mentions the Karst region as a planned transboundary biosphere reserve. However, no practical attempts in this direction are in evidence.

In the Bohemian-Bavarian Forest, trans-boundary cooperation plays an important role. Since the fall of the Iron Curtain this region has become a place where people from East and West Europe get together. Cooperation between the administrations of the national parks is not limited to scientific research. Transboundary cooperation in the region concentrates on the following fields:

- Visitor information: For instance, an information point was established at the border with bilingual information on landscape, nature and culture of the Czech and German parts of the region. This project was implemented by the two national park administrations. The information point was established in 1992 near a new pedestrian border crossing. In addition, the border control station in Bayerisch Eisenstein (D) houses an information centre which was established as a result of a common project between partners from regional Czech and German protected areas.
- Culture: A prominent example of good partnership between Germans and Czechs is the so-called 'glass ark' – a huge sculpture made of glass symbolising common nature and culture. Various cultural events accompany the glass ark in different locations of the two biosphere reserves. The project is financed by private and regional sponsoring, mainly from Germany and by the EU Community Initiative INTERREG III A.

- Strategic partnership: In 1999 a memorandum was signed by the national parks with the aim of strengthening cooperation and focusing work on special fields such as wildlife management, environmental education, as well as research and monitoring.
- Environmental-friendly transport: The successful public bus service of the Bavarian Forest, the so-called Igelbus, connects with the national park bus service in the Bohemian Forest. There is an agreement to connect the lines by similar timetables and good connection points. It is a well functioning system of public transport especially for visitors.

However, there has also been bad experience in both study areas. Language problems, cultural differences and prejudices have caused problems in cross-border cooperation. A further factor is also important in the examined regions, the resources available. The partnership between the biosphere reserves administrations can be described as unequal. In the Karst region, the Hungarian partner is much more powerful than the Slovak administration. Thus Hungarian actors give a good example in terms of commitment, but they are also able to dominate the work. As a consequence, there are more ideas for trans-boundary cooperation than concrete realisation. In the Bohemian-Bavarian Forest this problem is also familiar. The German Bavarian forest is better organised and has more experience in, for example, managing international projects. The administration has more financial and human resources to commit to international work.

4 Conclusions and outlook

The fact that the protected areas all have international approval as biosphere reserves is not sufficiently communicated within the areas. The opportunities offered by the biosphere reserve concept have not been sufficiently recognised by key actors in both regions. The protection category 'national park' is better known to the public, so that everybody can associate something with a national park. By contrast, the term 'biosphere reserve' remains mysterious for most people. In practical terms, the main task in the biosphere reserves under study is nature conservation, although the international biosphere reserve concept places greater emphasis on sustainable regional development. The traditional preserving approach of nature conservation dominates work in the protected areas.

However, there are many attempts that underpin the role protected areas can play as engines of cross-border development and cooperation. In this context, tourism is the most promising issue. There is a growing market for nature-orientated tourism, and the landscape of the biosphere reserves in question is very attractive. Their status as national park also serves a trademark for tourism, except for the biosphere reserve Slovensky Kras in Slovakia.

Large protected areas, and especially biosphere reserves, provide a concept for sustainable development. In implementing this concept they provide an opportunity for regional development, especially in peripheral areas situated at the border. Cooperation is an important factor in achieving this goal. The administrations of protected areas can help establish links between stakeholders at the regional level and across borders. Innovative ideas are needed that foster the idea of promoting economic growth while preserving natural resources. In this context, local inhabitants play an important role. The support and active involvement of local people is essential. Unfortunately, personal initiative is very low in the analysed regions. People must in future be encouraged to take part in decision-making processes and to establish an atmosphere that encourages creativity.

References

Europarc Federation (ed) (2001) Transfrontier Protected Areas. Europarc Federation. Grafenau

Evans DM, Henry IP (1995) Sustainable tourism projects: a transborder case study of Sumava National Park and associated landscape protected area, Czech Republic. In: Bramwell B, Henry IP, Jakson I, Guyet A (ed) Sustainable tourism management: Principles and Practice. Tilburg University Press, Tilburg, 201–216

Nolte B (2005) Tourismus in Biosphärenreservaten Ostmitteleuropas. Hoffnungen, Hindernisse und Handlungsspielräume bei der Umsetzung von Nachhaltigkeit. [Tourism in biosphere reserves of Central Eastern Europe. Expectations, obstacles and opportunities for the implementation of sustainability]. Mensch & Buch Verlag, Berlin

Sandwith T, Shine C, Hamilton L, Sheppard D (2001) Transboundary protected areas for pace and co-operation (Best Practice Protected Area Guidelines series, 7). IUCN, Gland, Cambridge

Tesitel J, Kusova D, Bartos M (2003) Tourists' Reasons for visiting mountain areas: a case study of the Sumava Mountains. Landscape Research 28: 317–322

UNESCO (ed) (2002) Biosphere reserves. Special places for people and nature. UNESCO, Paris

UNECSO (2006) List of Transboundary Biosphere Reserves. Available online: http://www.unesco.org/mab/BRs/TBRs.shtml, visited on 18.11.2006

Valenta M (1994) Sumava Biosphere Reserve. In: Jenik J, Price M F (eds) Biosphere Reserves on the Crossroads of Central Europe. Czech National Committee for UNESCO's Man and Biosphere Programme, Praha, 49–64

Environmental dimension of transboundary spatial development — driving forces in environmental regionalism

A case study on the Polish-German borderland

Marek Degórski

Institute of Geography and Spatial Organization, Polish Academy of Sciences, Warsaw

1 Introduction

The natural environment, and both geopolitical and economic activities are regulated by their own laws. This is due to the functional-structural organisation of nature and the cultural conditioning and development of socio-economic phenomena. Alas, the latter frequently conflict spatially with natural resources. One of the most striking examples is the incompatibility between the spatial distribution of areas of high natural value and administrative boundaries of different rank.

A big problem in environmental management is posed by ecologically valuable areas – with a significant potential of natural resources – that are divided by national boundaries. This problem becomes particularly difficult when the administrative border separates two countries with different political systems, cultures, histories, and levels of social development (Degórski 2002). Likewise, the attitudes of individual societies towards the problems associated with the natural environment, including perception of the human impact on the development, transformation and protection of the environment, often differ considerably (Hilden & Furman 2001).

In recent years, in the course of EU enlargement in 2004 and 2007, there has been significant convergence in concepts and directions of development in border areas between accession countries and the 'old' EU

Member States (Degórska & Degórski 2000, 2003). There has also been a pronounced convergence in the attitudes of the local communities towards the particular problems resulting from the functioning of the border zone, including the management of natural resources (Degórski 2005). More attention is being paid to assessing the influence exerted by human activity on the environment in the context of the rational use of natural resources as well as their protection. The activities prompted by this assessment are insofar alike on both sides of the border; joint projects thus become possible, which essentially affect the regional development policy of the entire border zone (Bijman 2002; Nijland 2005).

The quality of the natural environment constitutes a significant factor in the development of border areas, where high compatibility is needed in the use of natural resources, to be attained through joint efforts to determine management objectives for the ecological space, while common strategic goals begin to integrate the areas on the two sides of the border, generating a coherent ecological, social, and economic system. It is characterized by similar local and regional perspectives on both sides of the border, and by joint ventures and projects. These processes may lead to the emergence of so-called transboundary regionalism (Scott 1998, 1999), defined as a spatially integrated form of political, environmental, social and economic cooperation and problem solving. It transcends the limits of national administrative practice and attempts to create (or re-create, as the case might be) a sense of cohesion, interdependence and common interest across national boundaries.

The purpose of the present paper is to stress the importance of natural resources for the development of border areas and to answer the question whether the natural environment may constitute a driving force for the emergence of coherent border regions. The paper also analyses the external and internal conditions influencing the development of ecologically, socially, and economically coherent border regions. The example taken is the Polish-German borderland.

2 Institutional conditions for environmental management in the Polish-German borderland

Planning and management of the environment in border areas, as in other areas of a country, are subject to both international and internal regulations.

2.1 International institutional conditions

External conditions are constituted first of all by the international legal regulations and conceptual prerequisites for European Union ecological policy and bilateral agreements between neighbouring countries (Degórska & Degórski 2000; Williams 2000). International legal regulations can be divided into four groups:

- international treaties and conventions,
- European informal strategies or "soft laws",
- formally binding EU directives and
- bilateral agreements (Degórski 2005).

2.1.1 International treaties and conventions

Among the most important international agreements from the point of view of natural environmental systems are

- the Environmental Impact Convention in the transboundary context (1991),
- the Cartagena Protocol (2000) on biological safety, referring to the Convention on Biodiversity, and concerned with the transboundary movement of the modified living organisms,
- the Helsinki Convention (1992) on cross-border consequences of industrial catastrophes, and
- the Basel Convention (1989) on control of cross-border movement and removal of dangerous waste.

A dozen or more EU directives and associated by-laws should be added. The primary purpose of these documents is to optimize the use of the natural environment potential, to limit degradation and to protect its most valuable resources, and to make ecological policy coherent in the framework of bilateral collaboration and of the entire EU. The intention is also to facilitate solutions for individual sectors of transboundary ecological policy.

2.1.2 Informal European strategies or 'soft laws'

Examples of European documents with a more or less informal character are the Pan-European Strategy of Biological and Landscape Diversity (1995), the European Spatial Development Perspective (1999), the European Landscape Convention (2000), and the European Strategy of Sustainable Development (2001). These documents seek to achieve spatial development in line with the rules of sustainable development.

2.1.3 Formally binding EU directives

Usually they are concerned with sectoral tasks in which particular attention is paid to transboundary problems. Among the issues dealt with are:

- movement of waste (Council Directive 84/631/EEC of 06.12.1984, and its modification of 1986 – 86/121/EEC and 86/279/EEC), including also hazardous waste (Commission Directives 87/112/EEC of 23.12.1987, with an extension 90/170/EEC),
- integrated prevention of contamination and monitoring of the flow of contaminants (Council Directive 96/61/WE of 24.09.1996), and
- protection of the most valuable natural resources (Council Directive 79/409/EEC of 2.04.1979 on protection of wild birds, Council Directive 92/43/EEC of 21.05.1992 on protection of natural and semi-natural habitats of fauna and flora).

By virtue of the European Commission Decision 97/266 of 18.12.1996 concerning the definition of the scope of information on the areas proposed for entering the ecological system NATURA 2000, the latter has become the basis for establishing this system in the countries of the EU (Lanchbery 1998).

2.1.4 Bilateral agreements

They provide a governmental framework for collaboration between the two countries, e.g., the bilateral agreement between Poland and the Federal Republic of Germany signed in Schwerin on April 7th, 1994 (*Cooperation treaty between the government of the Republic Poland and the government of the Federal Republic of Germany*).

Other agreements have a more a local dimension, e.g., the agreement on cooperation between the two towns of Frankfurt/Oder and Słubice signed on 18th May 1993 (*Treaty between Frankfurt/Oder and Słubice on cooperation within the range of environmental protection*). This treaty includes provisions on the storage and segregation of garbage, carbon dioxide reduction and protection of the climate, inspection of combustion gas emissions and transport noise, protection of most valuable areas in consideration of the natural potential and common scenery.

2.2 National institutional conditions

Formal, legal internal conditions are determined by the regulations in force in the territory of a given country. In Poland they include acts of parliament (on nature protection, environmental protection and development, mining, treatment of waste, etc.), by-laws issued by the Ministry of the

Environment (particularly on the establishment of protected areas with a higher category of protection such as national parks and nature reserves, designation of Natura 2000 sites, protection of individual plant and animal species etc.), by-laws issued by other ministries (e.g. the Ministry of Agriculture), or motions passed by regional and local self-government bodies (establishment of legal protection entities of a lower category, like landscape parks, nature monuments, protected landscape areas), and numerous other regulations issued by regional and local administrative authorities. Similar legislation could be listed for the German side.

3 Environmental impact assessment as an instrument of environmental management in border regions

According to the European Spatial Planning Perspective (ESDP), the established directions of development of a given area are subject to environmental and territorial impact assessment. Environmental impact assessment (EIA) is defined as the analysis and evaluation of possible impacts on the environment of the proposed decisions or activities likely to cause significant effects on the environment. Assessment will help in arriving at informed decisions and setting development conditions. It serves as a basis for monitoring the implementation of decisions (NORAD 2003; SENSOR 2005). The present EIA provisions in Poland and Germany implement the EU Directive on Environmental Impact Assessment and the requirements of the UN ECE Convention on Environmental Impact Assessment in Transboundary Context (the Espoo Convention).

Throughout Europe, and hence in both Poland and Germany, the system of environmental impact assessment has become one of the tools of environmental management. Its purpose is to minimize conflicts between man and the environment. It encompasses a broad range of analyses of the potential consequences of a planned measure or project. These analyses are very often comprehensive, drawing on numerous partial analyses. The EIA, as a tool for optimising the environmental resource economy (used mainly to prevent adverse effects), is particularly useful in areas of high natural value or subject to major anthropogenic pressure.

Borderlands like those along the Polish-German border very often include areas that are valuable in terms of nature and which have also been strongly transformed by human activities such as the development of cargo terminals, border crossings, location of petty trade facilities (bazaars), intensified development of infrastructure etc. One of the basic challenges when elaborating a coherent EIA in bordering countries is to agree on assessment methods.

The use of EIA in border regions can reduce potential adverse effects on the environment which would otherwise result from certain projects and measures. This can contribute to the overall sustainable development of border regions. However, EIA is not a comprehensive tool in strategic regional development planning as it is undertaken only in connection with individual projects.

4 Natural resources and their role in the development of the Polish-German borderland

The application of EIA in planning and managing the environment not only significantly facilitates the assessment of human influence on the environment but also strongly enhances the effectiveness of procedures associated with the evaluation of environmental resources (Bródka & Macias 2006). Numerous authors point to these resources as important elements in regional development, generating its direction and intensity, accompanying many economic and social processes in the region, and consequently influencing the quality of the life of the local community (Young 1989, 1994; Barreda & Georgantzis 2000; Leibenath 2001; Degórski 2005).

When analysing the natural potential of the Polish-German borderland in terms of the set of factors essential for the development of the future of this region, we should state that the environmental resources do not differ much on the two sides of the border owing to the similar morphogenesis of the entire area and the associated morpho-lithological as well as climatic and biotic conditions. However, there are significant differences between different stretches of the border.

Water resources are among the most differentiated components of the environment in the study area. The worst hydrological conditions exist in the southern part (mountain and submountain regions) of the borderland. This is one of the areas poorest in water in both Poland and Germany while the best hydrological conditions pertain in the northern section of the border area.

Soils have evolved mainly from glacial and alluvial formations. Zonal soils, podzolic and brown earths, dominate, which quite unambiguously determines their medium or weak fertility. From the sanitary standpoint these are clean soils, 98%–100% in contamination classes zero or one for basic heavy metals (lead, zinc, copper, nickel and cadmium) (Degórski

2005). The most strongly contaminated soils (IV and V) are to be found only sporadically around power plants and metal works.

The biotic environment of the Polish-German borderland includes a major forest component, larger on the Polish side. The highest share of forest is in the central part of the borderland (Lubusza province — 48.8%, the highest in Poland). The ecosystems in a significant part of these forests have, however, been strongly transformed. The stands do not take full advantage of the fertility potential of the habitats and are primarily artificial. Compact forest complexes, most valuable in terms of biocoenoses, exist in the region of Sudety mountains, the Lower Silesian Forests, in river valleys, and on the island of Wolin (e.g., the Forests of Rzepin, Noteć River, Goleniów and Wkra River).

The symmetry of natural conditions on the two sides of the border means that planning the development of social and economic ties in the Polish-German borderland region must account for the possibility of competing economic activities, especially in farming and tourism, which can lead to innovation and efficiency. Thus, efforts should be made to create and strengthen complementary co-operative settings (Matkowski & Mazgajski 1996), which are already apparent at the local level in many places (e.g., Görlitz/Zgorzelec, Frankfurt/Słubice, etc).

The boundary between Poland and the Federal Republic of Germany is almost exclusively based on natural landscape elements such as rivers (Nysa Łużycka, Oder) and large water bodies (Szczecin Basin). The boundaries following the river courses are classified as integrating boundaries (Piskozub 1987; Matkowski & Mazgajski 1996) because the valleys as spatial units link the interests of the communities living on the two sides. However, the difficulty of socially integrating communities on the two banks of the border river is also often underlined (Kałuski 2000).

The concentration of settlements in river valleys, especially along border rivers, is historically conditioned. It results in growing care of the inhabitants for the quality of the river water and associated protection efforts, e.g., with regard to water uptake facilities and wastewater treatment systems (Berthelot 1997; Bijman 2002; Nijland 2005). Other joint activities of the communities living on two sides of a river are frequently directed towards developing navigation or constructing water engineering structures and bridges.

In the case of the Polish-German borderland, increasingly broad bilateral collaboration is taking place at the local level (e.g. Frankfurt/Słubice) or on a regional scale under external incentive generated by governance or EU regulation. It is often concerned with the water supply and treatment economy (Ciok 2003; Degórski 2005), the waste economy, air quality protection (Degórski 2005), and other forms of using the natural environmental potential and the cultural heritage for economic activation of the region (like the development of tourism, cf Liszewski 2003).

A particular instance of collaboration is the revitalisation of the palace and park complex established by Hermann von Pückler-Muskau and its opening for tourism. The complex is divided by the boundary which leaves the palace and its accompanying buildings on the German side and the larger part of the remnants of the English-styled manor park on the Polish side.

5 Development and protection of the environment in the Polish-German borderland

The Polish-German cooperation treaty defines the frame for joint sectoral undertakings, including environmental engineering and protection issues. The objectives are contained in three problem blocks including the following:

1. conservation activities,
2. logistical activities concerning the establishment of consistent protection goals according to international agreements, and
3. planning activities to establish a coherent system of planning and environmental management between the two neighbouring countries (Degórski 2002).

Legal protection of the most valuable objects of nature extends to 27.8% of the area on the Polish side (in terms of the total area of bordering voivodeships), and close to 20% on the German side (Igpik & Planco 1995). This continuum of areas featuring highly valued natural resources gives rise to a high number of activity and undertakings in bilateral collaboration, although there is still untapped potential for such collaboration, e.g., in regional development (Heimpold 2003) or in creating additional Natura 2000 sites on the Polish side of the border (MŚ 2006).

The WWF project “Green Belt of Oder and Nysa” is an example of Polish-German cooperation in nature conservation. It included the preparation of a pro-ecological development concept for the region and the establishment of protected areas along Oder and Nysa. The WWF, together with the Polish and German partners, succeeded to placing an additional 90,000 hectares under nature protection in the river valleys. The establishment of the National Park Warta Mouth and the Krzesiński Landscape Park can also be regarded as results of this project. Hence it was possible to salvage one of the most important ecological corridors in Europe.

There are proposals for intensified collaboration to meet the following challenges (Węcławowicz et al. 2005):

- Strengthening the supra-regional natural system of the Lower Oder and its tributaries by improving the natural coherence of the corridor formed by Oder and its tributaries and by protecting its landscape assets.
- Improving water quality and the water economy through municipal and supra-municipal programmes for water protection and through environmental management systems.
- Reclamation of former mining sites.
- Programmes for the re-utilisation of waste and its safe storage, along with the increase of its economic use.
- Constructing a modern, consistent system of flood protection by combining technical and ecological means, as well as (re-) constructing polders on German territory.

There is still major scope for environmental protection and resources use. It includes the establishment of transboundary biosphere reserves as on other Polish external borders (Breymeyer & Adamczyk 2005) or Transboundary Protected Areas for Peace and Cooperation (Sandwith et al. 2001). Such areas also give ground for building supra-national structures, linking cultural heritage elements of the countries involved, while providing presenting a regional identity.

Poland and Germany also collaborate in the "Oder-Regio" project for transnational flood protection in the Oder basin.

Polish-German agreements on environmental engineering and protection are reflected in the updating of plans and strategic analyses for the regions situated on the two sides of the border. They were also taken into account in Poland when updating the concept of national spatial development of the border provinces. And they played a role in the concept for spatial development of the country and the National Strategy of Regional Development for the years 2007–2013, as well as the National Development Plan for the years 2007–2013. Therefore it can be stated that the potential of natural resources, even if divided by the administrative boundaries of countries with different cultures, historical experience, and levels of economic development, can be correctly accounted for in the spatial economy of the border regions and can generate joint ecological, social and economic activities. This might become the driving force for the development of the entire borderland area in the two neighbouring countries (Degórski 2002).

6 Functioning of bordering areas in the context of transboundary regionalism

Tangible effects can be considerably strengthened through joint undertakings, i.e., symmetrical activities on both sides of the border. In the case of Poland and Germany, such joint initiatives have become much easier since the accession of Poland to the European Union because both countries are now subject to the same external formal-legal conditions. This facilitates the elaboration of joint projects for the use and protection of the most valuable natural assets, despite numerous formal-legal, social and economic differences which still exist between the two countries (Węcławowicz et al. 2005).

Closer collaboration in the border regions of two neighbouring countries creates mutual social, economic and ecological bonds, generating transboundary regionalism in all three dimensions, albeit conditioned by internal and external legal regulations.

7 Conclusions

The above analysis shows that natural resources are important factors in the development of border regions. They are on an equal footing with social and economic factors in stimulating regional development in the Polish-German borderland. It has also been shown that EIA is a very good tool for evaluating the state of the environment, both in terms of resources and changes conditioned by global trends (Sheppard 2005), and in terms of the human impact on these resources (Hilden & Furman 2001).

Polish-German cross-border collaboration in environmental management has led to numerous significant achievements such as the elaboration of a consistent system of protection for the Oder and Nysa valleys, the establishment of the International Park Lower Oder, improved surface water quality, etc. Nevertheless there is still important potential for developing this collaboration still further, for instance, in creating transborder biosphere reserves, international parks for peace, or a larger number of connected Natura 2000 sites.

References

Barreda I, Georgantzis N (2000) The interaction between economies and the natural space. In: Georgantzis N, Tarrazona B (eds) Spatial Economics and

Ecosystems. The interaction between economics and the natural environment. WIT PRESS, Southampton, Boston, 1–8

Berthelot Y (1997) Co-operation on transboundary waters. Natural Resources Forum 21, 83–84

Bijman S (2002) Dutch-German water management river Rhine. Four ways of transboundary co-operation for the design of transboundary management simulations. STORM Report Series 9. Available online: http://repository.tudelft.nl/file/428023/371625, visited on 09.02.2007

Breymeyer A, Adamczyk J (2005) Transboundary Biosphere Reserves at the Eastern end of the European Union: people and ecological dilemmas. Polish Academy of Sciences, UNESCO-MAB Committee of Poland, Warsaw

Bródka S, Macias A (2006) Etapy oceny środowiska przyrodniczego oraz ich znaczenie w procesie planistycznym [Stages of the assessment of the natural environment and their meaning in planner process]. Problemy Ekologii Krajobrazu 18, 57–66

Ciok S (2004) Pogranicze polsko-niemieckie. Problemy współpracy transgranicznej [The borderland Polish-of German. Problems of the transboundary cooperation]. Wydawnictwo Uniwersytetu Wrocławskiego, Wrocław

Degórska B, Degórski M (2000) Przestrzeń ekologiczna Polski w procesie integracji europejskiej [The ecological space of Poland in the process of European integration]. Europa XXI 5, 5–26

Degórska B, Degórski M (2003) The environmental dimension of European space according to the concept of trajectory. Europa XXI 8, 37–44

Degórski M (2002) Problemy regionalnej współpracy transgranicznej w aspekcie ochrony środowiska [Problems of the regional transborder cooperation in the aspect of the environmental protection]. In: Kitowski J (ed) Czynniki i bariery regionalnej współpracy transgranicznej – bilans dokonań [Factors and barriers of cross-border cooperation – Final report]. PTG, Rzeszów, 67–79

Degórski M (2005) Potencjał środowiska przyrodniczego oraz współpraca w zakresie jego wykorzystania i ochrony wzdłuż wewnętrznych granic Unii Europejskiej na przykładzie Polski i Niemiec [The potential of the natural environment and the cooperation within the range his utilizations and protections along internal borders of the European Union on the example of Poland and Germany]. In: Gworek B (ed) Obieg pierwiastków w przyrodzie [Ecological cycles in natural environment]. Monografie 3, 748–755

Heimpold G (2003) Zur Ausstattung der deutschen Regionen entlang der Grenze zu Polen mit wichtigen Wachstumsfaktoren [Location of growth factors in German regions at the Polish border]. Wirtschaft im Wandel 7, 215–221

Hilden M, Furman E (2001) Assessment across borders. Stumbling blocks and aptions in the practical implementation of the Espoo Convention. Environmental Impact Assessment Review 21, 537–551

IGPiK (Instytut gospodarski przestrzennej i komunalnej) & Planco (Planco Consulting GmbH (1995) Studium kierunkowe zagospodarowania przestrzennego obszaru wzdłuż granicy polsko-niemieckiej [The study of the spatial management of the area along the Polish-German border]. IGPiK & Planco, Warsaw, Essen

Kałuski S (2000) Border rivers and processes of European integration. In: Kitowski J (ed) Eastern borders of European integration processes. Papers and Monographs of the Department of Economy UMCS 19. Rzeszów, 83–97

Lanchbery J (1998) Long-term trends in systems for implementation review in international agreements on fauna and flora. In: Victor D, Raustiala K, Skolnikoff E (eds) The implementation and effectiveness of international environmental commitments. MIT Press, Cambridge, 57–87

Leibenath M (2001) Regionalmarketing als Instrument zur Entwicklung von Nationalparkregionen: Ergebnisse einer Untersuchung in der Müritz-Region [Regional marketing as tool for the development of national park regions. Results of a case study in the Müritz region]. Standort 25, 7–13

Liszewski S (2003) Możliwości i kierunki rozwoju turystyki w Dolinie Odry [Possibilities and directions of the tourism development in the Valley of Oder]. Łódzkie Towarzystwo Naukowe, Łódź

Matkowski R, Mazgajski A (1996) Przesłanki rozwoju społeczno-gospodarczego pogranicza polsko-niemieckiego [Premises of socio-economic development of the Polish-German borderland]. In: Chojnicki Z, Stryjakiewicz T (eds) Problemy współpracy regionalnej w Polsko-Niemieckim obszarze przygranicznym [Problems of regional cooperation in the Polish-German borderland]. Biuletyn KPZK 171, 43–57

MŚ (=Ministerstwo Środowiska) (2006) Specjalne obszary ochrony siedlisk NATURA 2000 w regionie kontynentalnym [Special areas of conservation NATURE 2000 in the continental region]. Available online: http://natura2000.mos.gov.pl/natura2000/pl/, visited on 12.02.2007

Nijland H (2005) Sustainable development of Floodplains (SDF) project. Environmental Sciences and Policy 8, 245–252

NORAD (=Norwegian Agency for Development Cooperation) (2003) Environmental Impact Assessment. Environmental Co-operation. Norwegian Ministry of Environment, Oslo

Piskozub A (1987) Dziedzictwo polskiej przestrzeni. Geograficzno-historyczne podstawy struktur przestrzennych ziem polskich [The heritage of the Polish space. Geographical-historic bases of spatial structures of Polish earths]. Ossolineum, Wrocław, Warsaw

Sandwith T, Shine C, Hamilton L, Sheppard D (2001) Transboundary protected areas for pace and co-operation (Best Practice Protected Area Guidelines series, 7). IUCN, Gland, Cambridge

Scott J (1998) Planning co-operation and transboundary regionalism – implementing European border region polices in the Polish-German context. Environment and Planning C, Government and Policy 16, 605–624

Scott J (1999) Comprehending transboundary regionalism: developing an analytical domain for comparative research. Paper presented at the RSA International Conference "Regional Potentials in an Integrating Europe"

SENSOR (= Sustainability Impact Assessment: Tools for Environmental, Social and Economic Effects of Multifunctional Land Use in European Regions) (2005) Sustainability Impact Assessment: Tools for Environmental, Social and Economic Effects of Multifunctional Land Use in European Regions (Newsletter 2). ALTERRA & ZALF, Wageningen, Müncheberg

Sheppard R (2005) Landscape visualization and climate change: the potential for influencing perceptions and behaviour. Environmental Science and Policy 8, 637–654

Węcławowicz G, Degórski M, Komornicki T, Korzeń J, Bański J, Śleszyński P, Soja R, Więckowski M (2005) Studium kierunkowe zagospodarowania przestrzennego obszaru wzdłuż granicy polsko-niemieckiej [Study of the spatial management of the area along the Polish-German border]. Institute of Geography and Spatial Organization, Polish Academy of Science, Warsaw

Williams P (2000) International law and the resolution of Central and Eastern European Transboundary environmental disputes. Macmillan, Basingstoke

Young O (1989) International Cooperation: Building Regimes for Natural Resources and the Environment. Cornell University Press, Ithaca, NY

Young O (1994) International Governance: Protecting the Environment in a Stateless Society, Cornell University Press, Ithaca, NY

The role of special economic zones in the socio-economic development of Poland's border regions

The case of the Kostrzyn-Słubice Special Economic Zone

Michał Dolata

Adam Mickiewicz University, Institute of Socio-Economic Geography and Spatial Management, Poznań

1 Introduction

Special economic zones (SEZ) are parts of the territory of a country in which legislation has created more advantageous conditions for pursuing economic activities than in other areas (Gwosdz et al. 2005: 18). As economically privileged areas, SEZ are a tool of regional policy, a form of economic and financial intervention by the government in the economy, and a new economic institution stimulating regional growth (Sowiński 1998: 140).

The main purpose of special economic zones is to accelerate economic growth on a regional scale. It is assumed that the economic growth resulting from the operation of SEZs occurs not only in a zone itself, but also outside its borders and contributes to the economic activation of the region. In accordance with the principles of economic and spatial policies, special economic zones should be established in both:

- areas offering unique comparative advantages (e.g., some border regions) with prospects for accelerated growth and maximisation of economic effects, and

- those areas especially hard hit by economic crises, where SEZs are primarily expected to reduce unemployment and restructure old industrial districts (Stryjakiewicz 1999: 91).

As the Polish experience shows, special economic zones are set up as a form of economic activation tool in regions whose economies require thorough restructuring and the involvement of external strategic investors, their capital and technologies. The chief inducement for investors, and also a privilege, is an income tax relief dependent on investment costs incurred or number of jobs created, as well as exemption from local taxes.

The operation of special economic zones leads to favourable economic changes in the host region. They include:

- technological progress in the region,
- an increase in exports,
- higher competitiveness of goods produced and services offered,
- efficient use of existing industrial assets and economic infrastructure,
- creation of new jobs, and
- development of natural resources while preserving the principles of ecological balance (*Special Economic Zones Act 1994,* Law Gazette no. 123).

The main aim of the present article is to define the role of special economic zones in the socio-economic development of Poland's border regions.

According to Chojnicki (1998: 11), a border region "is a territorial component of the given state or country which shares a boundary with another state and which is situated on one side of the boundary". The effect of the boundary on the development of a border region depends on its character as a barrier or link, as well as on its role in mutual interaction.

In Poland, special economic zones are located in border regions for two reasons:

- A SEZ situated in a border region acquires a location rent which offers it a chance for dynamic growth owing to possible links with the neighbouring country and activities in the economic and social spheres.
- A SEZ activates the economy of its border region, which had been poorly developed owing to its peripheral location under the centrally planned economy under political conditions relying on a tight closure of national boundaries.

Between 1995–2004 fourteen special economic zones were established in Poland, of which five lie close to a national border.

The frontier SEZs include:

- Kostrzyn-Słubice,
- Kamienna Góra,

- Wałbrzych,
- Suwałki, and
- Warmińsko-Mazurska (see fig. 1).

This period embraced two stages in the development of SEZs in Poland. The first involved establishing the legal and organisational conditions for economic activity, basic infrastructural investment, and issuing business permits which led to an inflow of investors. The second stage started with the actual launching of first enterprises in the zones. It should be emphasised that the planned level of economic activity and employment in the zones had not yet been achieved in 2004.

The present study consists of a case study of the Kostrzyn-Słubice Special Economic Zone (KSSEZ) situated in Poland's western border region. It focuses on the genesis of the zone, the mechanism of its operation, economic effects observed so far, and specific features of its growth and impact.

2 The Kostrzyn-Słubice Special Economic Zone

2.1 The genesis and growth factors of the Kostrzyn-Słubice Special Economic Zone

The KSSEZ was established on 15 November 1997 for a period of 20 years. It was supposed to initiate the formation of a growth pole in the poorly developed frontier Lubuskie region, embracing at that time the Gorzów and Zielona Góra voivodships. KSSEZ development plans expected the zone to bring about an economic upswing by:

- creating some 10,000 new jobs and reducing unemployment,
- stimulating manufacturing and service activities, and
- diversifying economic activities in the region.

The plans provided for the promotion of the zone in Poland and abroad, the attraction of investors, the establishment of cooperation between the zone and domestic and foreign economic organisations. Preference was given to activities employing advanced, environment-friendly technological solutions, cooperation with economic entities doing business outside the zone, and development of services for investors located in the zone.

Figure 1. Special Economic Zones (SEZs) in Poland

The KSSEZ was set up in a border region likely to attract investors due primarily to the zone's advantageous location on the western national border and the existing transport network. Gorzów and Zielona Góra voivodships, located on the outer limits of the European Union, were recipients of the most massive assistance under the EU border-region support programmes (PHARE CBC). When the KSSEZ was established, the Lubuskie region already had well developed transborder cooperation structures in the form of two Euroregions: Pro Europa Viadrina and Spree-Neisse-Bober. Since 2004, the Lubuskie voivodship has been a beneficiary of the chief assistance programme for border regions, INTERREG III A. The individual KSSEZ subzones were located in the vicinity of road and railway routes and the concomitant border crossings. These are the international highways E30 (Berlin-Poznań-Warsaw), E36 (Berlin-Wrocław) and E65 (Świnoujście-Szczecin-Gorzów Wielkopolski-Zielona Góra-Prague), as well as the Berlin-Warsaw railway line and the Oder Railway Trunk Line (Katowice-Wrocław-Szczecin).

2.2 The growth of the Kostrzyn-Słubice Special Economic Zone from 1997 to 2004

In accordance with its founding act[14], the KSSEZ covered 457 ha in two municipalities: Kostrzyn on the Odra and Słubice, which are its two subzones. The Kostrzyn subzone was composed of a few enclaves in the municipality (town) of Kostrzyn on the Odra. The Słubice subzone embraced a compact, undeveloped area located outside the limits of the urbanised zone of Słubice town, on the margins of the Rzepin Forest, near highway E30 (no. 2) and the border crossing at Świecko.

The KSSEZ is geographically dispersed. From the very beginning of its existence it showed marked spatial growth expressed both as an increase in its area and in the number of subzones situated in successive municipalities of north-western Poland. In this respect, the period 1997–2004 can be divided into the following two subperiods of KSSEZ development:

1. The years 1997–2004, when there was only a slight increase in the zone's area (to 463 ha), while the successive subzones were established exclusively within the boundaries of the present Lubuskie voivodship, i.e., in the municipalities of Gorzów Wielkopolski, Gubin, Nowa Sól, and Bytom Odrzański.

---

[14] The Council of Ministers' Ordinance of 9 September 1997 "On the establishment of the Kostrzyn-Słubice Special Economic Zone" (Law Gazette of 31 October 1997).

2. The years 2004–2005. In 2004 the total area of the zone grew considerably to 543 ha (fifth place in the country), while new subzones were set up also outside the boundaries of the Lubuskie voivodship, namely in the municipalities of Barlinek, Karlino and Goleniów in the Zachodniopomorskie voivodship. In 2005 the KSSEZ expanded even further to reach 805 ha, largely though the establishment of successive subzones in the voivodeships Lubuskie (Zielona Góra and Czerwieńsk), Zachodniopomorskie (Police), and Wielkopolskie (Poznań, Swarzędz and Chodzież).

Any increase in the area of the KSSEZ was not possible before 2004 owing to the provisions of the amended *Special Economic Zones Act* of 2000, which disallowed the expansion of SEZs in Poland[15]. In 2004 an increase in the area was made possible to meet the needs of large investors, and it was those that had set up in the KSSEZ.

The first licence to carry on business in the KSSEZ was issued on 15 October 1998 to Podravka Poland Ltd. in Kostrzyn on the Odra. Between 1998 and 2004 the KSSEZ issued a total of 81 permits, with the biggest number in 2000 (45). As is the tendency in Poland, the number of permits issued much exceeds the number of valid permits and, even more so, the number of economic entities actually operating in the zone. Thus, at the close of 2004 the number of valid permits (50, second place among the border zones) amounted to 64% of those issued (81). In the KSSEZ the first firm (Podravka) launched its activity on 1 July 2000; by the end of 2004 the number of enterprises active in the zone had grown to a mere 16 (fourth place among the border zones). Of the enterprises doing business in the zone, 11 were medium-sized (50-250 workers), four were small (up to 50 workers), and only one (Faurecia Gorzów) had more than 250 workers. Of the 34 firms issued with a valid permit but which had not started operations by the end of 2004, ten were medium-sized and the rest small.

In 2004 total capital invested in the KSSEZ amounted to 844 million PLN (seventh place in Poland and second among the border zones), of which foreign firms accounted for 95.1%. Among the KSSEZ subzones, Kostrzyn came first in terms of investment volume (65% of total investment in the Zone). In terms of the origin of investors, the leader was Italy (47.0%) followed by France (29.2%) and Croatia (8.3%). The share of investors from neighbouring Germany was 7.2%.

An analysis of investment outlays by size of enterprise and industry, as of September 2004, revealed a characteristic feature of the KSSEZ: 71% of investment was made by small and medium-sized enterprises. By comparison,

[15] Cf. The Act Changing the Special Economic Zones Act and some other acts of 16 November 2000 (in force since 1 January 2001).

the average contribution of SMEs to total investment was 56%, in the remaining border SEZs and a mere 42% in the interior zones. In the KSSEZ, 78% of the investment figure was accounted for by firms in the pulp-and-paper and plastics industries, which shows the specialisation of the zone.

In 2004 the enterprises operating in the KSSEZ employed a total of 1,753 persons. All the jobs in the KSSEZ are so-called new jobs. This is a distinguishing feature of zones established in areas with a low level of urbanisation and poorly developed industry. In other SEZs in old industrial districts (Mielec, Starachowice, Tarnobrzeg) the proportion of new jobs ranged between only 50% and 90%.

2.3 The role of the Kostrzyn-Słubice Special Economic Zone in the development of its border region

Analysis of the effects of the KSSEZ on the socio-economic development of the border Gorzów subregion embraces two issues: (1) the contribution of the firms located in the zone to the economy of the subregion, and (2) their impact on local labour markets. The study covers the period from 2000 (the start of operations by the first enterprise in the zone) till the end of 2004.

The effect of the KSSEZ-based enterprises on the labour market was determined by the three types of unit in the territorial division of the country, i.e., the subregion, poviats (counties) and municipalities covered by the Zone. The basic index adopted here was the proportion of industrial employment in the zone to total industrial employment and to total overall employment of the given territorial unit.

In 2000 Podravka Poland Ltd., the first enterprise to open in the KSSEZ, employed 100 people in Kostrzyn on the Odra. This was a mere 6% of total industrial employment and 2.5% of total employment in the town. In 2001 KSSEZ-related employment grew to 550 people, of which 93% was accounted for by Kostrzyn-based firms (the début of ICT, Teleskop, and Agro-Bor Luisa). Employment in the Kostrzyn subzone rose then to 33% of total industrial employment in the town. At the same time the first enterprise made a start in the Słubice subzone with a staff of 40 (Konecke Ltd.). In 2004 the 16 firms active in the KSSEZ employed a total of 1,753 people in three municipalities of the Gorzów subregion: Kostrzyn on the Odra, Słubice, and Gorzów Wielkopolski.

In the light of the above analysis, one can conclude that between 2000 and 2004 the effect of the KSSEZ was significant only on the local labour markets (municipality level) of Kostrzyn on the Odra and Słubice, where zone-based firms accounted for 39% and 41% of total industrial employment, respectively. On the larger labour market of Gorzów Wielkopolski (a total employment of 34,000), the two big KSSEZ-based enterprises accounted for 5% of total industrial employment. At the level of the Gorzów and Słubice poviats, the contribution of zone enterprises to total employment did not exceed 10%, and to industrial employment 19% and 13%, respectively, while in the Gorzów subregion their role was insignificant (see table 1).

Table 1. Employment in the KSSEZ and the proportion of total employment of selected territorial units of the Gorzów subregion (as of 31 Dec. 2004)*

Subregion, poviat, commune	Overall employment			Industrial employment		
	Total (persons)	KSSEZ	proportion of KSSEZ (%)	Total	KSSEZ	proportion of KSSEZ (%)
Gorzów Poviat	9365	857	9.2	4497	857	19.1
Słubice Poviat	8820	329	3.7	2486	329	13.2
Gorzów Wielkopolski	33865	567	1.7	11040	567	5.1
Gorzów subregion	75371	1753	2.3	28743	1753	6.1

* Without employment in enterprises with up to 9 persons. Source: Own compilation on the basis of data from the Ministry of the Economy and Labour and the Statistical Office in Zielona Góra.

The limited effect of the KSSEZ on the labour market was reflected in the persistence of a high unemployment rate in the Gorzów subregion in that period. During the first four years of KSSEZ operation (2000-2004), a marked increase in the unemployment rate was recorded in all the three poviats where zone-based enterprises were sited: in Gorzów and Słubice poviats from 21% to 26%, and in Gorzów Wielkopolski from 20% to 24%.

3 Conclusions

In conclusion, the contribution of the KSSEZ to the industrial development of the Gorzów subregion between 2000 and 2004 can be described as significant, although there were only 16 active enterprises out of the 50 that have valid permits and have declared their intention of starting operations.

Over the next few years the KSSEZ to play an increasing role in the economy of the Gorzów subregion. What the KSSEZ has not notably improved is the labour market situation in the area.

The case of the KSSEZ reveals two aspects in the operation of border SEZs. First, the development of SEZs established 'from the ground up', (i.e., greenfield investment) in areas of poor infrastructure and no industrial tradition is a long-term process. Seven years after its establishment, the KSSEZ had failed to achieve the targets set in its development plan. By 2004 a mere 17.5% of the targeted number of jobs had been created. Secondly, it turns out that the location rent resulting from a zone situated in a border region is no guarantee of dynamic growth. In the KSSEZ a mere 7% of investment came from Germany, while strategic investors came from more distant countries of the European Union.

References

Chojnicki Z (1998) Uwarunkowania rozwoju regionu nadgranicznego – koncepcje i założenia teoretyczne [Framework conditions in border regions – Concepts and theoretical requirements]. In: Gruchman B Parysek J J (eds) Studia rozwoju i zagospodarowania przestrzennego [Development studies and spatial planning]. Wydawnictwo Akademii Ekonomicznej, Poznań, 11–48

Gwosdz K, Jarczewski W, Huculak M, Wiedermann K (2005) Specjalne strefy ekonomiczne w Polsce. Założenia a praktyka [Special economic zones in Poland. and practice]. In: Domański B, Gwosdz K (eds) Dziesięć lat doświadczeń pierwszej polskiej specjalnej strefy ekonomicznej. Mielec 1995–2005 [Ten years of experiences with the first Polish special economic zone. Mielec 1995–2005]. Instytut Geografii i Gospodarki Przestrzennej Uniwersytetu Jagiellońskiego, Agencja Rozwoju Przemysłu S.A. Oddział w Mielcu, Kraków-Mielec, 17–37

Sowiński R (1998) Specjalne strefy ekonomiczne jako instrument gospodarowania przestrzenią Polski [Special economic zones as an instrument of Polish spatial planning]. In: Parysek JJ, Rogacki H (eds) Przemiany społeczno-gospodarcze Polski lat dziewięćdziesiątych [Social-economic change in Poland in the 1990th]. Bogucki Wydawnictwo Naukowe, Poznań, 131–144

Stryjakiewicz T (1999) Adaptacja przestrzenna przemysłu w Polsce w warunkach transformacji [Adaption of industrial areas in Poland under framework conditions of tranistion]. Wydawnictwo naukowe UAM, Poznań

V Conclusions

Bridging the gaps?

Cross-border governance between top-down policies and local needs and limitations

Markus Leibenath[1], Ewa Korcelli-Olejniczak[2], Robert Knippschild[1]

[1] Leibniz Institute of Ecological and Regional Development, Dresden,
[2] Institute of Geography and Spatial Organization, Polish Academy of Sciences, Warsaw

1 Exploring the horizons

The contributions in this volume shed light on various aspects and levels of cross-border governance and sustainable spatial development in Central Europe. In this final chapter, the editors attempt to summarize the main findings and propose some directions in which further research could move.

Miosga's article in the first section on external influences and framework conditions highlights the shift of emphasis in European and German spatial development policy – away from integrative approaches placing equal weight on economic, social and environmental concerns towards the priorities of the Lisbon Agenda, which centres on economic growth and the creation of new jobs. This tendency has to be regarded as an imminent threat to peripheral regions and to sustainable development in its original sense. Although European cohesion policy for the years 2007-13 features "territorial cooperation" as one of its three major objectives, the funds earmarked for cross-border cooperation will be allocated in proportion to population, which is a disadvantage for sparsely populated regions. However, time will show if and to what extent lagging border regions are able to benefit from this concentration on metropolitan regions and growth poles.

Ciok and Raczyk take an in-depth look at the practical implementation of one specific European regional policy tool in Poland's western provinces: strand A of the Community Initiative INTERREG III. They have found the bureaucratic procedures to be overly complex and the bulk of money going into large infrastructure projects at the expense of smaller projects and other sectors. Of course it has to be taken into consideration that INTERREG III A was a novel funding tool for Poland and that operating procedures had to established and tested, but by the same token Ciok's and Raczyk's findings clearly indicate what has to be changed to improve the sustainability of cross-border cooperation.

It is revealing to compare the two contributions in the book's second section on cross-border governance at the regional level. The analyses show that European funds can be a facilitator of cross-border governance but have to be complemented by a number of other factors if enduring self-governance is to be achieved in cross-border regions. These other factors include a certain degree of institutional depth, social capital, as well as cooperative attitudes on both sides of the border – to mention just a few. The case study on the Rhine-Scheldt Delta demonstrates that the European integration discourse – the mere debate about European integration and the spreading of respective ideas – is equally or maybe even more important as a driver of cross-border cooperation than European funds (cf. Leibenath 2007). This conclusion is supported by Deppisch's finding that INTERREG money induced no more than a 'grant coalition' in the Euregio Via Salina.

The three papers in the section on cross-border co-operation between cities and metropolitan regions all deal explicitly or implicitly with the question "Why cooperate?" The reason for not doing so are plain to see: long distances to span in the case of Warsaw and Berlin, differences in economic weight and power as in the case of Bratislava and Vienna, and administrative, mental and historic barriers in the second case study on the German-Polish-Czech Triangle. With this in mind, it is evident that cross-border cooperation is by no means a matter of course. All three authors – Piotr Jaššo, Knippschild and Korcelli-Olejniczak – discuss the potential benefits of cooperation. In the case of Warsaw and Berlin which Korcelli-Olejniczak examines, there are synergies and complementarities in the field of culture and city tourism. Jaššo points to the necessity for both Vienna and Bratislava to compete internationally for investment and tourists and to the fact that this challenge can be mastered best if the two cities pool their efforts to make the most of their assets. With transboundary twin cities the situation is different again, because such cities are dependent on each other in so many areas of daily life, such as urban infrastructure, waste disposal and housing – to mention just a few, that cooperation does not need much justification. However, Knippschild's distinction between the results and benefits of cross-border cooperation cannot be made from the outside: it depends on the perspective taken by those involved in the cooperation process or affected by it and on the values of the espouse. What for some is but a mere result may for others be a tangible benefit. Likewise, it is hardly possible to prescribe a certain level or degree of co-operation externally. There may be many good reasons for cooperation and integration, but border cities may have equally good reasons to opt for competition instead – at least in some fields of urban policy.

The four papers in the last section examine cross-border cooperation in the sectors of transport, nature conservation, environmental protection, and the economy. What these contributions elucidate is, firstly, that there are specific pressures on the sustainability of border areas, resulting, e.g., from changing traffic patterns due to EU enlargement and the implementation of the Schengen Convention. Secondly, the contributions of Komornicki, Nolte, Degórski and Dolata highlight some of the strengths and weaknesses of border regions, the opportunities and threats they face with regard to sustainable development. Many border regions are only sparsely populated, are home to endangered species and offer high potential for recreation. At the same time, they are often economically lagging regions, whose natural assets are endangered by increasing streams of vehicles and tourists. Thirdly, the contributions emphasize the importance of sector-specific institutions such as biosphere reserves with their staff and budget. Poland's special economic zones, many of which are located close to national borders, represent another specific type of institution that is designed to foster the economic performance of disadvantaged regions. And finally, as Degórski points out, there is European legislation such as the directives on Environmental Impact Assessment (EIA) and Strategic Environmental Assessment (SEA) that impose requirements for transboundary coordination and can thus contribute to a more sustainable development of border regions.

2 Lessons learned

The papers included in this volume cover only a few examples from a wide range of potentially relevant issues and topics. Nevertheless they provide an impression of current research on cross-border governance and sustainable spatial development.

The contributions identify some gaps in current approaches to cross-border governance and sustainable spatial development in Central Europe.

Indeed, the differences between regions, contexts and scientific perspectives might appear so large that, at first sight, it seems difficult to find any common ground.

Yet there is one issue running through almost the entire book: the influence of EU policy on cross-border governance and, in particular, the EU enlargement of 2004. While the enlargement had physical effects such as changing patterns of transboundary traffic and the opening or closing of checkpoints at the borders of new Member States, it did also impose a fundamentally different institutional framework for cross-border cooperation. This applies both to funding schemes such as INTERREG and its successors and to various legal provisions for cross-border cooperation and coordination, but also to the changing discourses of European integration.

The external conditions for cross-border cooperation are continuously changing and evolving as we can see in Miosga's paper. Furthermore they are embedded in national institutions through which they are implemented and which account for many national particularities in terms of organization and thematic priorities as Ciok and Raczyk show for some the Polish INTERREG III A programmes. However, the final effects of these Europeanizing influences can only be understood as the results of an intricate interplay of actors, institutions, and discourses at European, national and local levels.

When looking at the grassroots of cross-border cooperation, Ciok and Raczyk as well as De Vries and Deppisch interestingly – and maybe surprisingly – agree on the limited outcome of the Community Initiative INTERREG III A in terms of enduring transboundary governance structures and sustainable development. This finding is basically supported by Leibenath's analysis of a large cooperation project that has been funded through another European programme. The reasons for this lack of success appear to be

- that the actors at regional and local levels pursue their own agendas which are often not in line with the priorities of the European Commission. As a result, e.g. the INTERREG III A funds for Poland have mainly been channelled into infrastructure projects with questionable relevance for cross-border cooperation and the sustainable development of the respective regions.
- that the regional INTERREG III A communities are but poorly connected to other relevant border-straddling organizations and networks.
- that in some regions the structural and institutional conditions are generally unfavourable for cross-border cooperation because e.g. of an lack of trust and social capital like in Deppisch's case of the Austrian-German Euregio 'Via Salina'.

3 Quo vadis? – Perspectives for further research

The authors that have contributed to this book volume have, with only few exceptions, conducted single case studies. This is to a certain extent typical for research on cross-border governance and spatial development. It was only recently that larger scientific endeavours with a broader empirical base have been launched, e.g. the EXLINEA project which was funded under the 5th European Framework Programme (cf. Scott 2006). Yet much work remains to do to broaden the empirical base of border research. Hence a first recommendation for further research is to compare different cases with similar contexts, e.g. from the same region, or relatively homogenous cases from different contexts, e.g. in the field of transboundary spatial planning. To this end cross-cultural research teams would be of great help.

Thus far nothing has been said about promising questions for further research or about relevant theoretic strands to be taken up. While there is of course a multitude of potential research perspectives, only a few selected ones which are particularly important from the authors' viewpoint will be discussed in the following.

To begin with a fundamental question: Is a focus on national borders still appropriate? Or to put it differently: What heuristic value has the very notion of borders to offer? The importance of national borders is at least in Central and Western Europe diminishing, although many Central European borders still mark severe economic and cultural disparities which – from the viewpoint of territorial and social cohesion – call for political and scientific attention. Political power is increasingly shifting away from national governments to European and international organizations or it is devolving to regional and local levels, whereas some European policies in turn require transboundary cooperation and coordination at regional level. The relevance of the jurisdictions of public entities such as nation states is also decreasing because business and civil society organizations, both of which are often multi-national in nature, are gaining ever growing political influence. In federal countries like Belgium or Germany, where entire policy fields such as nature conservation, spatial planning or culture are almost entirely in the hand of sub-national legislative bodies, boundaries between the component states are almost as important as the federation's external borders. Multiple, overlapping fragmentation of jurisdictions, legislation, physical networks, economic relations, cultures, languages, and identities are a generic feature of modern societies. Some fragmentation coincides with national borders while much does not. This being the case, there is hardly any approach to shaping the physical environment that does not have to cross borders. Much of the literature on actor networks, interagency cooperation, regimes, and coalition-building is actually about crossing borders in policy-making. Further research on cross-border governance and sustainable spatial development could therefore benefit from a broader concept of borders that encompasses other types of boundaries besides national borders. Such research should address the significance and the function of borders and how people perceive and deal with them.

This leads directly to the consideration that borders cannot be regarded only as physical realities or as a preordained phenomenon: they are man-made phenomena. Border-related research in the field of spatial development and planning, in particular, often still approaches borders from a positivist standpoint proceeding on normative assumptions about the benefits of cross-border cooperation and integration. It is exactly in this vein that van Houtum's dictum of "moral geography" (van Houtum 2000: 63) has to be read. Against this backdrop it can be concluded that research on border regions and transboundary planning should leave the trodden path of positivism and embrace post-modern approaches inspired by constructivism. This would enable researchers to better incorporate different perspectives, for example, from different levels of policy-making, different countries and different scientific disciplines. There are undoubtedly gaps between all these categories and perspectives. However, science can hardly bridge them, but should rather contribute to identifying them and enabling actors to reflect upon them.

A constructivist approach could also be helpful in tackling the issue of sustainable development. Sustainability is addressed by many actors, usually supportively. But people inevitably differ in their understanding of sustainability. For instance, Macnaghten a. Urry (1998: 232) have fittingly noted that "ordinary people" are rarely interested in the abstract principles of sustainability as laid down in political declarations. Instead, they have a strong motivation to preserve their immediate quality of life and improve the conditions of their residential environment. Therefore it would be worth while to investigate:

- who raises the question of sustainable development of border regions
- who means what by "sustainability",
- what factors hamper the sustainable development of border regions and
- how these obstacles can be overcome.

These proposals having been made, it should be noted that notion of "border region" is also questionable. Of course border regions can be distinguished from other types of region by their proximity to certain boundaries such as national borders. However, if one takes the plethora of boundaries and the decreasing importance of individual demarcations into consideration, it has to be asked whether "border regions" should not be defined in terms of features other than, for example, the mere existence of a national border. In many instances it would be more significant to base classifications and comparisons on criteria such as accessibility, proximity to metropolitan regions, natural assets, economic structure, prevailing modes of governance in a specific sector, existence of certain institutional arrangements, and the like. In other words, national borders do not necessarily constitute a meaningful type of region, and much that is discussed under the heading of "development of border regions" would be better discussed in more specific contexts, such as transport, conservation, infrastructure, etc.

A final remark on the practical relevance of border research: The scientific investigation of spatial planning and sustainable spatial development, in particular, should address problems and issues of high practical relevance. This implies, on the one hand, the existence of strong policy-science interfaces. On the other hand, efficient science-policy interfaces are needed to ensure that research findings feed into policy-making and planning circuits. For example, Leibenath & Knippschild (2005) have documented the role researchers can play in evaluating the processes of cross-border cooperation through active participation. There are certainly many other ways in which scientists can improve the practice of cross-border planning and development. However, the bottom line is that such research should be both theoretically well-grounded and relevant for practitioners.

References

Leibenath M (2007) Europeanization of Cross-Border Governance? – A Case-study on the Cause, Form and Consequences of a Cooperation Project in the German-Polish-Czech Border Triangle. Space & Polity 11: 151-167

Leibenath M, Knippschild R (2005) Systemic Evaluation of Cross-border Networks for Actors: Experience with a German-Polish-Czech Cooperation Project. Journal of Borderlands Studies 20, 73–90

Macnaghten P, Urry J (1998) Contested Natures. Sage, London

Scott JW (ed) (2006) EU Enlargement, Region Building, and Shifting Borders of Inclusion and Exclusion. Ashgate, Aldershot

Van Houtum H (2000) An Overview of European Geographical Research on Borders and Border Regions. Journal of Borderlands Studies 15, 57–83